BISON
BOOKS

LYNETTE PERRY AND
MANNY SKOLNICK

Keeper of the Delaware Dolls

University of Nebraska Press
Lincoln and London

Publication of this
volume was assisted by
The Virginia Faulkner Fund,
established in memory of
Virginia Faulkner, editor-in-chief of
the University of Nebraska Press.

Congress Cataloging-in-
Publication Data: Perry, Lynette, 1914–
Keeper of the Delaware dolls /
Lynette Perry and Manny Skolnick.
p.   cm. ISBN 0-8032-8759-3
(pa.: alk. paper)
1. Perry, Lynette, 1914–   .
2. Delaware Indians—Oklahoma—
Biography. 3. Delaware Indians—
Oklahoma—Social life and customs.
4. Oklahoma—Biography.
I. Skolnick, Manny, 1946–   .
II. Title. E99.D2P46   1999
976.6'004973—dc21
98-39896   CIP
[B]

To Gordon Perry—
my husband,
my strength, my love.
Wherever you were,
there was home.

CONTENTS

ILLUSTRATIONS

Following page 102

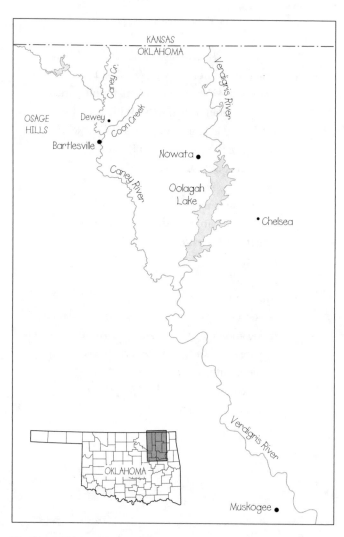

Northeast Oklahoma

Keeper
of the
Delaware
Dolls

INTRODUCTION

I want to start off by saying that I'm not the kind of person who thinks my life is so important that it needs to be in a book. Which may seem a strange thing to say, since you've just opened a book coauthored by me, giving an account of my life. I haven't written this because I think the events and adventures I've lived through are so out of the ordinary or so fascinating that they cry out to be recorded. Not at all. I would say, instead, that my experiences represent a way of life that's pretty much passed from the American scene.

I grew up in rural Oklahoma at the time when Indian Country was moving into the twentieth century. I think the things I've seen and done are pretty similar to what many other people who grew up in the little river communities of eastern Oklahoma lived through. If they'd written about their lives, I probably wouldn't have written about mine. But I do believe this is a story that needs to be told. Time has made many of my experiences, commonplace when they occurred, seem exotic. I don't want them to pass beyond exotic to forgotten.

I believe the world I grew up in has something to say to the very different world I've aged into. You can decide whether I'm right, or merely sentimental, as you read this reminiscence. One thing I've learned in the process of growing old is that the past lives in the present. We're where we are because of where we've been. I think that's especially true of the relation between native and white, which is still central to the American experience, though most people may not think so.

For all that, I probably wouldn't have written this book if my daughter Linda, with help from her husband Manny, hadn't first produced her story of growing up in the Oklahoma Indian child welfare system. Even though I adopted my girls directly from the Murrow Indian Orphanage, there were many things about their lives there that I didn't know until I read her book.

I've always liked to tell my girls little stories from my own experience, partly because I think some of the people I grew up with really were larger than life. Some years ago, I took to writing my grandchildren poetic letters praising the pleasures of the country. Linda saved those letters and started telling me I should write a book about my family, my growing up — that sort of thing. It got to be kind of a running joke between us. Linda would say, "Ma, we've got to get started on that book." I'd agree. Once or twice she went so far as to get me a tape recorder, but it never went beyond that. I don't know why; I just didn't believe it was really possible, I guess. I mean, who was going to publish a book by an obscure rural woman who'd lived her whole life within fifty miles of her home place?

When Linda and Manny wrote their book, everything changed. It became clear that you could tell a modest but important story, and if you told it well, you might be lucky enough to find a publisher who believed in it. I also found that my son-in-law was someone who could get into another person's skin, understand their thoughts and feelings, and tell their story as they'd want it told.

So when Linda and Manny asked me once again to consider writing a memoir, I had to give it serious thought. We decided we'd get started and see how things went. We scrapped the tape recorder and relied instead on another newfangled invention—the telephone.

Our biggest obstacle was distance. The kids live in Chicago, 650 miles away, so we couldn't just sit down and talk things over the way I'd like. But the phone proved to be a suitable way to proceed, and I think we did manage to get the story told just about as well as it could be. It probably helped that Manny and I have known each other for more than twenty years. He's pretty familiar with these parts too, having visited upward of forty, fifty times. And he has Linda right there with him; she keeps me sharp and jogs my memory when it gets a little fuzzy.

Let me say a little something about memory. I'm eighty-two years old now. I think my recall is pretty good. But I'm not going to tell you I remember conversations that took place seventy years ago. On those few occasions when we do re-create a conversation, we're trying the best we can to give you a feel for the talk as far as I can remember it. The look and feel and sound and taste of things are here to the best of my ability to make such things come alive. I suppose some of the other participants might remember events differently. That's unavoidable. Like in that Japanese movie, *Roshomon,* where everybody remembers the same events so differently. And in that case there weren't decades and decades between the facts and the remembering.

The way we did this book was that Manny and Linda and I got together at the beginning and decided what the highlights, the chapters, should be about. I wanted to spend the most time on my childhood, because that's what interests me most and I think will intrigue you. When I was growing up there were still stomp dances and Indian football games that brought the Delawares and Cherokees together on a Saturday evening; you could still hear the tribal languages spoken along with English; the Peyote

Church held its services alongside the Christian denominations. The cultures were in an uneasy balance; the native heritage was still evident in the land.

After we agreed on our outline, Manny called me from time to time. We'd talk about one chapter, then he'd remind me what our next topic would be so I'd have a chance to think about it and sharpen my memories before we talked. He sent me a set of chapters as he finished them. I read them through several times. Then Manny and Linda drove down, and we went through the book page by page, while I added and took away, suggested changes, and made sure everything was just as accurate as could be.

Manny took the suggestions back with him and made changes as he thought proper, then we went through the manuscript again. I'm satisfied now that *Keeper of the Delaware Dolls* presents those things that were important in my life about as well as I'm able. I hope it holds your interest and gets you thinking about a way of life that prevailed in my part of the country not so very many years ago.

The Long
Road Home

One

SPINNING MEMORIES

I sit on my front porch, just outside the circle of brilliant arc light that has replaced my Gordon as my guard against the dread of dark.

I look down a shadowy expanse of lawn to the rural road that is my lifeline to Chelsea and Nowata and points beyond. It is a road much traveled. I follow headlights from the east, knowing they've driven up the Parker hill and down the Lucy Lewis in the dark. I watch cars coming from the west that have roared past Allen's Point and crossed the moon-bronzed waters of Oolagah on an earthen dam. I can close my eyes and see the seven miles of this most familiar road that runs on to the east, and the seven to the west, that they have yet to travel. I don't know where the cars will go when they turn onto Highway 28 or Highway 169. It doesn't matter, for the moment they draw lines of light on my eye, they become a part of my world, a fleeting memory.

I sit with my daughter and son-in-law, who have urged me to make a record of that world of memory and have offered to help me with the daunting task. We've spent many pleasant evenings on this porch, sharing talk to the rhythm of summer winds that rustle the branches of my lovely crape myrtle, bathing us in its sweet perfume. Bees and wasps buzz sleepily among the lavish red and pink and white blossoms. Their droning sounds like snoring.

Overhead is a dazzle of stars, so brilliant that the herky-jerk of bat flight is visible against them. If these two, my children, were with me every evening, I would shut off my arc light and restore the night. But they aren't, so I accept the necessity of my lamp. It is a lesser evil, better than the fear it protects me from.

Overhead also, much nearer, unseen in the dark, is a canopy of spiderwebs. I know they're there, out of sight, and take comfort in the knowing. Some of the webs anchored to my porch roof boast diameters as wide as the full span of my arms; big webs woven by fat red spiders, thick as my thumb.

I've come to appreciate spiders—patient, industrious creatures with a job to do. I admire their tenacity; I've watched their labors with pleasure as they throw their flimsy-strong silk threads into the teeth of the wind again and again. It must be some sort of creativity that drives them to their labor. I hope so; the idea pleases me.

I believe God rejoices in his creation. That he has been so generous as to allow some of his creatures—not just us humans—to taste that joy. Beavers, surely; also the wasps, bees, spiders that share my porch at night.

I number myself in that company. I've created some things in my long life that delight me, made them for that reason and no other. Paintings: a few canvases in my house, the altarpiece for our Winganon church. And dolls; I think I like my dolls best of all the things I've made with my hands. Four stand on the shelf in my living room where I keep my treasured things—two old Delaware ladies in ribbon dresses, a girl dressed in buckskin. Those and my Grandma Wahoney doll. How hard I worked on Grandma, to make her features just exactly like the ones that look out at me from old brown photos, ninety-year-old photos. Features that could have been carved from some hard, fine-grained wood—thin lips, the lower one pushed out, defiant. Wise, hard eyes. A face aged past personality. A face that has seen, suffered, endured, accepted.

I'm proud of that doll. Of all the things that comfort me in my old age, she's especially dear. It'll take me a while to get to the point where I can really explain why. But you'll be meeting her again—her and the wise old woman she stands for in my mind. In fact, Grandma Wahoney's the focus of this first part of my story—Grandma and the traditional Delaware lifeway she represents.

It occurs to me that Grandma should be with us as we sit in my favorite spot to talk about my life, my memories. So I bring her doll out to the porch. Without making a show of it, I lift her up in the dark, up toward the spiders. They work to create their worlds; Grandma did that too. I suppose the same can be said of me, a maker of dolls.

There's another reason I'm running on about spiders. The land I live on, the land I know as well as most people know the rooms of a house they've long lived in, is interlaced with threads of memory. My memories and those of other old ones like me.

Like spider silk, these threads of memory are tough and fragile both. I'm eighty-two years old, and I know that wind breaks spiderwebs. My kind of webs, too. It has happened to enough of us already, old ones like me, children of the Delaware and Chero-kee and Osage settlements, whose personal webs of memory are blown away by a wind that I don't think I have to name. I know it has always been this way, must be this way; and I am content with that knowledge.

And yet, when my children suggest that my memories can be traced, can be recorded, can outlive me, I'm willing to hope it may be true. I think of it as a duty I owe the land I've loved. A duty

I owe the life I've lived. A defiance that may parallel the spider's defiance in daring to spin her web. A devotion that may equal the devotion of countless natives before me who structured their worlds with legends and history stories. Like them, my landmarks are marks on wampum belts, to aid my memory. Like them, I am part of the places I've lived in, and they are part of me.

What does this web of mine look like? The answer in detail is this book. But the short answer is that it follows the pathways I've taken in my life to all the meaningful places—the foot trails and dirt tracks, the gravel and paved rural roads, the highways and interstates. These paths radiate out from the places I've called home, the towns, the centers. If you traced them out on a very detailed map, they might look a little like a spiderweb.

My web of memory has two centers. One of those is the Perry farm, west of Chelsea, east of Oolagah, very near the rumor of a town called Winganon, without a post office or gas station, but with one church and one bait shop. This is the place where I've lived my adult life.

The other center is my old Delaware home place, near the historic frontier town of Dewey and the once-glorious center of oil wealth, Bartlesville. My home place can be found on property owned by my nephew, Les Reynolds, but it is not touched by any mapped road. Hidden in woods beyond pasture, along a stream that flows fresh and sweet only in memory, my home place is marked by shards of pottery and gravestones too weathered to read. I'm not sure if Les can find it without my help; soon its human history will be entirely effaced by nature. Soon, but not now. I still remember.

Grandma Wahoney knew our Delaware home place, walked its woods, drank its waters. When we travel back to visit it, we go also to visit her. Let's be on our way; Grandma's waiting.

Two

YOU CAN
GO HOME AGAIN

People tell me I don't drive quite as well as I used to. People who love me tell me that, so I suspect it may be true. It doesn't matter though, not for this journey. I can drive this road in my sleep. I really think that once I steer my Buick down my rutted dirt driveway and turn right toward Oolagah, the car could find its way on its own, at least to the old town of Dewey. From there even I have to check my mental road maps; it's been a long time.

It seems there are many remembrances of things past along my road. So many bittersweet reminders of good times long gone. Even in rural America, where the past endures in countless, careless keepsakes scattered over the land, the march of time is relentless. What we don't maintain succumbs to the forces of nature, to growth and decay, as immune to sentiment as the greed and ambition of a big city developer. The stone walls of our little Waller School rise on my right — massive, yellow, weathered, not yet tumbled by tornado. The old country school, where I cooked lunch for fifty children — all our Waller children — stands empty, dark, lonely. It is home to birds and bats, who accept its shelter now. The schoolyard, which rang with the laughter of kids at recess, is a long time silent. It strikes me as morbid. I wish there were some use we could put the old structure to, but nature has too strong a hold on it now; renovation would cost too much.

I think it stands now just to remind me, and a handful of other old ones, of days when the rural communities, hardly towns, took care of their own needs. When the last of us goes, and that will be soon enough, it will have no reason to stand. If God is paying attention, he'll send a tornado then to erase Waller from the landscape. Or he'll just trust the rain and grass roots to do the job.

Oolagah has been here about thirty years now. It's a massive lake for this once-dry part of the Plains—twenty-five miles long, a couple wide at the widest—that dominates our piece of Oklahoma. Sometimes when I drive along in a daydreamy mood, the lake surprises me. I see its expanse of muddy-dark water, a few trees, still green, protruding from its shallows, and think to myself, now what the heck is that doing here? What used to be a fertile plain, rich bottomland, blooming in corn and cotton and the salad crops—lettuce and poke and turnip greens and tomatoes and green beans that farmers would truck over to town or to vegetable stands along the highways—is all under water. Lovely groves of the best pecan trees are submerged, their bounty drowned, their slim, straight trunks standing like soldiers in the night dark of that muddy lake. Trim little whitewashed farmhouses, the ones the owners were too feeble or heartbroken to move, lie dreaming under Oolagah's brooding waters.

Egrets, snow white and elegant, bob on gentle waves to my right. A flock of bulky white pelicans that flew the long course of the Arkansas River up from the Gulf flap and fret to my left. A buzzard sweeps the sky in slow, graceful circles high above the squabbling pelicans, waiting for one to drop the cargo of small fish that bulges its heavy pouch. There are no cars on the road; the soft rustle of waves rises up to meet the silence of the blue sky. I stop my car on the earthen bridge, as I do sometimes when no urgent mission presses me on, to enjoy nature's little dramas.

The buzzard is joined by another, then a third. Their lazy circles intersect; dancing shadows fall on the pelicans, wheeling, pirouetting, drawing tight and tighter. The big birds grow agitated, as if the high shadows are whips. One after the other the pelicans break away from the lake, rising from the water with power and startling grace. A few drop morsels of food from their bulging bills. The buzzards, great wings tilting almost imperceptibly, drift down in tightening spirals, as if flying down tornado funnels. They skim across the water, plucking bits of fish out of the lake. It's a triumph for the buzzards, yet harmless enough; the pelicans hold food enough in their pouches to satisfy even their enormous appetites.

The place where the pelicans gathered soon empties; water covers over the recent tumult as it always does; calm returns. Calm suits that particular spot. It's not easy to be sure about these things, but the best I can figure it, the pelicans were swimming just above Bullet Ford.

Bullet Ford. We passed some lovely summer afternoons swimming there—my girls and I, my great friend Shug Hayes and her two kids. It was back when Oolagah was a gleam in the eye of some army engineer. Back when the Verdigris River wound its way through a fertile valley, now drowned. We'd finish the chores and bundle the kids into one of our cars. You couldn't drive all the way to Bullet Ford, but close. The last couple hundred yards was on a footpath, winding through thickets of chokecherry and wild plum.

Bullet Ford was a bend in the river where the swift waters slowed, where no boulders troubled the current with white water, where ledges of smooth rock rose up from midchannel in regular steps, even up past the shoreline. We could spread our towels on beds of water-smoothed sandstone. We'd lie in patches of shade cast by the overhanging trees if we needed to escape the fierce summer sun. Or if we wanted to work on our tans, we'd lie in the hot-bright spots of our rocky leopardskin. The children would wade and splash in the shallows. Shug and I littered the approaches to the deep channel with sinkholes and quicksand and treacherous currents; our stories guarded the kids and gave our watchful eyes some rest. In our defense, we knew there were deep holes in the riverbed somewhere off Bullet Ford. The muddy brown water ran swiftly as it rounded the bend; the currents could eddy and swirl. Even quicksand—my mother told me stories of cattle being sucked down by the shifting sand in local rivers and creeks, bellowing and thrashing until their muzzles sank below the surface, then sending up a cascade of bubbles. Come to think of it, she may have told me the same scare stories I told my girls. You know, they seem to work.

Bullet Ford was a place for stories. You could find things at Bullet Ford, things that whispered of extraordinary happenings. Arrowheads for one, beautifully worked flints. Lance points too—knives, scrapers, the whole native arsenal. Sometimes we sent the kids looking, or Shug and I would hunt for them. We took scores of flints out of that place, and it seemed there were always more to be found. You had to wonder why. Was it some sort of mine? A chipping station? Maybe there'd been a battle—long forgotten, among natives, before the Trail of Tears and all the migrations shuffled Oklahoma's Indian deck. Or perhaps, when the great herds lumbered choking and bellowing across the Verdigris, hunters waited on the far shore to strike through a tumult of flashing hooves and deadly horns. Stone points thrust between third and fourth rib to the heart, or hunter dead.

I could lie on the flat, hot sandstone bed, head pillowed on my rolled towel, turn a flint in my fingers, and imagine a past beyond the possibility of knowing.

There were other things, too, whispering their own stories at Bullet Ford. Bullets, of course, most of them new make, hunters' bullets. But now and then an old, lumpy lead poured by hand in some frontier mold turns up among the river gravel like a frozen tear from a killing time.

Now and then the land opened to reveal a rarity. One was a Peace Medal; it was the prized centerpiece of my friend Ruthie's collection. I saw it only once, but it made an impression, and I think I remember it pretty clear.

A Peace Medal . . . from Andrew Jackson. Andy Jackson, frontiersman, Indian fighter, father of the democracy . . . and of the Trail of Tears, profiteer from the sale of Cherokee land, seventh president, implacable enemy of all Indians everywhere. Jackson issued "Peace Medals" to the chiefs he cowed and humiliated. Some cruel instinct for irony, I guess. The medals were witness to the benevolent intentions of the Great White Father, visible symbols of a native prayer for peace and a remembered white pledge of peace.

It turns out that Indian memories are harder, longer lasting than the silver of this medal. The shells that make up our Delaware wampum are more durable than that silver. A record of every treaty, every land sale, every ceremonial where one of our hopeful, foolish sachems received a Peace Medal from that hickory-hearted hand is woven into a wampum belt. Somewhere, behind museum glass or in some dim-lit basement, the wampum commentary on this particular discarded medal, recording season and moon of its gift and receipt, hides away. I wouldn't be able to read the wampum; I don't know who could read it anymore. But I have seen the medal. On one side an Indian and a white hand clasped in friendship. On the other, Andy Jackson's profile and signature. There was a hole near the top, I remember, where some sort of ribbon—red, white, and blue probably—was passed.

We Delawares were delighted, so it seems, by gleaming medals and gaudy ribbons. But our sachem, who carried his promise of peace from Pennsylvania to Ohio to Indiana to Missouri to Kansas to Oklahoma, must have thrown his medal away at last. I can imagine his pain of heart when, the last treaty broken, the boundaries of the Cherokee Nation opened with all the others to the Sooner land rush, the old man understood at last that they were all, all the white men, Andy Jacksons.

Enough of that. This is not about politics, simply a drive down memory lane. But they are all—politics, history, true memory—interwoven like the strands of a wampum belt. There is no politics worth anything without accurate history. And history is nothing more or less than the collective memory of people like me. But we have a destination, modest and personal, and it's time to get back in the car and head on down the road.

I shortcut around Nowata. For us country folk even this little town is traffic—a couple of stoplights, a major intersection, a corner hedged by honeysuckle where the local constabulary lurks to waylay speeders. I prefer the back roads, though there's still a stretch where you learn to ease up on the gas pedal.

Highway 60 cuts through ranch land, running a gauntlet of barbed wire straight on to Bartlesville. On a clear day you can see Blue Mound out on the horizon. Once you know its name, you see it in a sort of bluish haze. I've asked people who didn't know the name if they noticed anything odd about the distant hill. They say one thing or another, but hardly ever that it looks blue. I've always known it as Blue Mound; it's always had a bluish look for me.

There's something about humankind that just doesn't like flats, it seems to me. Anyway, that's my explanation for mound building. I believe many of the little round-top hills poking up from the Oklahoma grassland are man-made, are Indian mounds. Of course some, Spiro chief among them, and Blue Mound too, incontestably are just that. Others . . . I suppose the archaeologists would give me an argument about them. But that's neither here nor there. Blue Mound, rising a couple of hundred feet above the plain, is the biggest footprint that native people — any people — have put on this land.

You can't climb Blue Mound anymore; not if you're regular folks, at least. Not for thirty years or so. Property rights prevail, even on a native place a thousand years old. And the owners don't seem to want us up there anymore. It was different when I was growing up. Not much fence on the range then. Nothing to slow us down. When my brother Henry and I got the notion to explore around Blue Mound, there was nothing in our way. Open range to ride, just a couple of gates to lift and latch.

We'd mount up and ride over to the mound when we wanted a certain kind of adventure. For us, Blue Mound wasn't about long-forgotten Indians. It was about outlaws of recent vintage, the desperadoes who had fled U.S. law to hide out beyond its reach in Indian Territory. Some were men of fearsome reputation and terrifying deeds — bank robbers and murderers who were the bogeymen in our parents' scare stories. Because Blue Mound could be seen from afar, it was the place for far-seeing. From its commanding heights, outlaws could scan the plain, keeping a lookout for pursuing posses or rogue lawmen like Rooster Cogburn, who might well disregard Cherokee sovereignty in pursuit of bad men. Such monsters as John Wesley Hardin, whose tally of victims surpassed Billy Bonney's, if his reputation back East did not, had used the mound to hide and headquarter, in blatant disregard of whatever might be termed authority.

We came, Henry and I, to find the leavings of outlaws. We dug and sifted the dirt of Blue Mound, uprooted sage along with less pungent weeds and grasses to see what the roots might have caught. We found a bullet casing here and there that we could not be persuaded had come from so prosaic a source as hunters. We hid away those shells, convinced they were relics of a yesterday when our humble corner of Oklahoma had been frontier wild. Once we found a belt, the leather chewed almost to ribbons by coyotes, only the heavy steel buckle intact. We brought it home, of course, hid it in a secure nook near our home place, visited it to reaffirm the bond of a shared secret. I don't know what became of it at last; if I were to search carefully enough, the buckle might be recoverable still.

Blue Mound disappears from my rear window; Bartlesville, and beyond it the quainter charms of Dewey, are just down the road. There are many, family and friends, I might visit in these dear, familiar towns. There are shops, restaurants, museums with fond associations. Above, in the Osage Hills, wild mustangs graze the prairie grass. Frank Phillips's wonderful Woolaroc ranch has long been a refuge for my family and me, as well as for the deer and cattle and bison and ostriches and mountain sheep that wander its grounds. Before black gold built its kingdom here, this was Delaware country—the piece of the sovereign Cherokee Nation that my wandering tribe negotiated for our use when the winds of history blew us, with so many others, into Indian Country.

We're getting close to the Whiteturkey home place now. Leslie, my nephew, my sister Betty's boy, lawyer for the tribe, rodeo cowboy, owner of a sweat lodge, occupies the family allotment now. There's something in the air here that's unlike any other place. It may not be so for you, but it is for me. I don't exactly smell it, but I feel it in my nose, my lungs, my blood. It awakens me.

One more ghost of memory to visit before we reach Leslie's driveway. This one is a real ghost. At least that's what it says in a long-ago issue of the *Bartlesville Examiner*. You could look it up, except I can't remember the date anymore—not even the year.

It was on this same road, if it was the same road when it had no asphalt, only dirt. The grandfather of this road, I suppose. My brother Henry saw it; my papa was almost victimized by it.

I remember the night Henry came roaring up to the front door, faster than ever before, in his rattletrap Ford. He rushed in bug-eyed, out of breath, locked the door and pulled the drapes. He'd seen something; worse, it had chased him down the road. A fog, a wisp of smoke, undoubtedly a ghost . . . and the faster he drove, the faster it followed. Papa smiled, shook his head. It was a clear-sky, full-moon night, he explained to me later. The old Model T belched exhaust—in the moonlight, a ghost.

My aunt Shirley was also in the room that night. She was a local newspaper reporter. Apparently she didn't make the same connection with smoke and moonlight. She brought Henry's story back to her newsroom; from there it made its way, unexamined, to the pages of the *Examiner*. The Delaware ghost that could run right along with a Model T. The Jim Thorpe of ghosts. It was a story that bewildered and intrigued. Apparently it also angered and terrified.

A week later, Papa had forgotten all about Henry's speeding ghost. He rode home alone, as was his habit, along our rural road. It was a stormy evening, and he wore a yellow rain slick. Maybe he whistled as he hurried his horse toward the dry comfort of home; he did that sometimes. More likely he rode in the silent company of his thoughts. He must have been preoccupied, because he didn't notice the mob that had gathered down by the creek until he'd ridden almost into their midst. He estimated the crowd at five hundred, most of them men, most of them armed, all of them terrified. They were there to hunt Henry's ghost, and my father, dressed in his yellow slicker, emerged to fill the bill.

Fortunately Papa was well known in those parts, and a quick thinker and good talker to boot. The air filled with the click, click,

click of men cocking rifle hammers. It sounded like a swarm of locusts feeding, as he remembered the scene. It was up to him to defuse the situation.

"What's going on here tonight, George?" Papa asked a neighbor he recognized in the gloom. He spoke in a remarkably even voice given the circumstances—at least it was even in the retelling.

"Ghost about," George answered in a voice cracking with excitement, as Papa impersonated it. "Been scarin' folks. And we're here to stop it."

"Now, let's not lose our heads here, George." Papa was the voice of reason. "You ever see a ghost wearin' a rain slick?" Well, no, of course not. The logic was unassailable. The men uncocked and lowered their pieces. Papa made his way home.

The hundreds of ghost hunters, who must have been a sizable chunk of Bartlesville's male population, hung out by our creek for a week or so. My dad in his yellow raincoat was the closest thing to a ghost they ever saw. Gradually their numbers diminished; finally, ghostlike, the last one slipped away into the night.

Ghosts of memory linger along the road to my home place. One wears a yellow rain slick. None pose any threat; the danger is in the forgetting.

Three

ACROSS
TWO CENTURIES

Her Delaware name was Ma Wah Taise. Mine is Pima Pen Okwe. We never touched, Ma Wah Taise and Pima Pen Okwe. Though she lived to the enormous age of 108, she was five years in the ground before I came into the world. Between us, two old women, our lives span very nearly all of two centuries, save for the interlude 1909 to 1914. When she was a girl, Indiana was a haven beyond "civilization" for the shattered tribes of the Atlantic Coast. Now, when I'm an old woman, it seems there is no haven on this earth beyond the reach of the same manifest destiny. Two women. Two centuries. A connection.

Although I came to this world too late to see Ma Wah Taise in her leathered skin, she was present in my life from earliest memory. Four generations removed, she was my Grandma Wahoney—the name she picked up in a marriage to one John Wahoney somewhere in the long middle years of her life and carried ever after.

For me, she is all the generations of Delaware women. Her daughter, Akweapailu, is a name scratched on a stone marker, then erased by weather—nothing more. Her granddaughter, Lisey Whiteturkey, is a single poignant mother memory—a deathly pale young woman glimpsed from the porch as the flame of her life blows out, in a matter of days, extinguished by what was then called galloping consumption.

Lisey was removed from her home and housed in a tent out of terror of the disease that choked her lungs. Grandma Wahoney nursed her, easing Lisey's suffering as she could; ninety-year-old Grandma, rendered by long life immune to the power of plague. The disease ran its course, and my mother, little Phoebe, kissed and cried Lisey into her grave.

Grandma came to the young widower, Sam Whiteturkey, with an offer. "Let me raise Phoebe as mine. You have three others, burden enough. I can teach her our talk and the work of a Delaware woman. One day I'll be too old to live alone. She'll be a strong young woman and I the one who'll need looking after." It didn't happen quite that way. Grandma, who went into the forest to cut her firewood and carried it out on her back when she was 90, did the very same thing when she was 108. But perhaps she knew it would be that way even when she asked Sam for his help.

So Ma Wah Taise became mother to my mother. Phoebe Whiteturkey was raised as Delaware women had been raised a century before, in Indiana, when Grandma was a girl. My own ties to the old Delaware ways are memories and stories—the same ties that have bound our people each to each since the beginning. Probably I'm one of the last in the line of Delaware legend and memory. My own ties run only through Grandma Wahoney by way of a mama who wanted to share what she knew was a remarkable legacy. When I was a little girl, I was curious and eager; later, when I could have asked to more purpose, I was deep into the day-to-day of my life and missed my chance. My mother died, her story and Grandma's story lost except for tatters that cling to my memory. I don't want to lose those.

I know Grandma Wahoney only at the beginning and the end of her life. It seems that when we're near to the birth and dying times we're also nearest to the essence of ourselves.

Some say that Grandma was a lost daughter of the Wyandots, taken in and raised by the Delawares. The history is possible; Delawares and Wyandots were neighbors along the Ohio and again in Indiana territory. Families shattered, children were lost and found, and those found were welcomed into whatever home found them. But there may be something else at work here. It seems to me that one pattern of belief, common to many cultures, has the hero come from outside the group. Perhaps something like that is at work in the notion that Grandma Wahoney, the model of a Delaware matriarch, should have begun her life as a Wyandot.

Wyandot or Delaware at birth, Ma Wah Taise was Delaware when she first became the heroine of her legend. She was on a horse behind her mother, the two of them riding through the woods. It was spring: the meadows were sweet with new grass and budding flowers, the thawed ground thick with mud, the streams boiling with floodwaters. I can picture her perched firmly on the bare back of an Indian pony, wrapped in a blanket, her arms tight about her mother's waist, the wind in her hair, her mother's voice crooning in her ear. To ride alone together in the breathing silence of the springtime woods, touched and quickened by sunlight along with the young leaves and featherless birds, is to share a life-giving intimacy.

And then, a river to be crossed. It may have been the White River, the string along which the Delaware towns in Indiana were hung like beads. Or it may be some other; it is not named in the story. Banks were eroded by the swift current, here and there breached by the floodwaters to form cold, shallow ponds with sucking mud bottoms. It was a dangerous crossing, but in this place and time such dangers were the condition of living. They were not sought, foolhardy, but neither were they shirked. The Delawares have lived along streams always; they know and respect rivers but don't fear them. So mother and daughter urged their sturdy pony on.

It may be that a long crossing of muddy shallows weakened their mount, or the current may have surprised them with its fury. The horse slipped and plunged; the girl slid off into swirling waters. She watched her mother, clinging to the horse's neck, disappear into the terror of their drowning. The people found mother and horse some days later. They didn't find the girl—Grandma as a girl—for weeks after that.

They found her, when they did, on an island. The floodwaters had made their way down the White to the Wabash, the Ohio, the Mississippi and into the Gulf by that time. Grandma was well and strong, and she had a story to tell.

As the waters made ready to swallow her, Ma Wah Taise felt something lift her under her arms and at her head. She reached out and grabbed onto what seemed to be a thick rope. Swimmers had hold of her, and she clasped them close. They were, it seemed, about as tall as children—as she—with stout arms and legs. The one who cast her a rope turned back to her and smiled. She was biggest of all, with long soft hair, a brown wrinkled face, narrow crinkly eyes, and a button nose—she must have looked something like Grandma's own photos a hundred years later. The swimmers pushed, pulled, and dragged her to her island. When she got ashore, she saw that the rope in her hands was really a tail, the long, stout tail of an otter.

The largest of the swimmers spoke a strange language that Grandma somehow understood. "I am Otter Woman," her rescuer said, "and I've taken you to my island. You will be one of my children until your own people find you. My children know no hunger, I promise you." Then she dived into the river, splashing and cavorting in the water like any ordinary otter. Otter Woman was as good as her word, bringing fresh fish nearly every day. She introduced a tiny man, very neatly dressed in a little spotted coat with a tidy little collar on the back. Tiny Man Woodpecker moved on and off the island just as if he could fly. He brought the girl sticks for her fire and seeds, fruits, and nuts to eat. Sometimes he drummed a rhythm on a hollow tree, and Grandma danced her loneliness away. Otter Woman witnessed the last dance. "Your people will come for you soon," she said. "You will live to be an old woman. We will see each other only once more. A year before your time is over, I will come again to you. And you will know." Then she slid into the brown water and vanished.

When the men of our tribe at last pulled their dugout canoes onto the island and found Grandma, they were astonished to see that the little girl was plump and healthy. She told them about all the help Otter Woman and Tiny Man Woodpecker had given her. The Delaware elders listened and nodded. We were a river people; the ways of Otter Woman and her friends were known to us. She had saved our children before, and they had always grown to become special people. When Ma Wah Taise returned to her village, there was no shortage of families who wanted to raise her.

That was the story Grandma told my mother. It was not, however, the only version that has reached my ears. Grandma Wahoney became a legendary figure in northeastern Oklahoma — the old woman who knew healing arts — and the tale that foretold her prominence was related by many. I've heard that it was a mermaid, not Otter Woman, who carried the drowning child to safety. The mermaid version seems wrong to me, culturally; I've never heard of mermaids in other Delaware stories. I suspect they came over on the *Mayflower*. But it's certainly true that we'd lived with the whites for three centuries, time enough for mermaids to be adopted by my people, along with rifles and beads and metal skillets.

I hold with the version I've told you here. The thing that decides me is that the description of Otter Woman and the photo of Grandma in her last years look alike. The wrinkled old woman with her narrow, burning eyes and neat little nose came to look a little like her rescuer. It seems so absolutely right to me. I can't imagine Grandma ever looked much like a mermaid.

The next eighty-five years of Grandma's life, before she took Phoebe Whiteturkey into her home, I can only guess at. I know that to get to our Oklahoma home place Grandma walked the longest road of anyone in this book. Call it the Delaware road. It wasn't a straight one. It had its share of tears, like the more famous Cherokee trail, and it ended in the same place. It started in Indiana, and from there to Missouri. Missouri to Kansas. Kansas to the Cherokee Nation in Indian Country. Which became Oklahoma without another move being required.

The people got to be pretty good at picking up everything they could carry and moving it a couple of hundred miles farther on into that elusive and shrinking refuge from the white man's destiny. Grandma's first trek began in 1820, when some 1,300 Delawares, with slightly more horses, hauled and carried all their portable treasures in crowded wagons, covered and uncovered, two hundred miles to the town of Kaskaskia, Illinois. The strongest among them walked. Grandma, at nineteen, always tireless, was surely one who walked.

At Kaskaskia they waited days, even weeks, to be packed into long flat-bottom boats and ferried across the Big Muddy. History tells us that the chaotic crossing over a swift, mile-wide river panicked many of my people. I hardly believe it. From what I know about the Delawares and rivers, it makes no sense. Maybe it was trusting to white conveyance that scared them, I don't know. I'm sure Grandma was unafraid. She may have kept an eye out for Otter Woman, though. And given her connection with the tribe of strong swimmers, the fearful probably gathered round her in a tight, strained knot during the crossing.

Missouri and Kansas proved to be Indiana all over again: conflicts first with the tribes native to the region and then, shortly after, with the flood of white settlers that followed hot on Delaware heels. Missouri was a decade, no more. But in that time we made an enemy who would deal Grandma a heart-hurt years later. Game was scarce, and Delaware hunters ranged far and wide, even onto the Plains, in search of the remaining deer and buffalo. They breached the hunting grounds of the Osages, who ranged from the big river west to the Osage Hills and the short-grass prairie beyond. Hunting parties met, clashed, killed; revenging war parties sacked Delaware and Osage towns. The government stepped in and brokered a treaty between the tribes, but the blood feud simmered.

Sometime during the long middle years of wandering, the four-plus decades in Missouri and Kansas, Grandma Wahoney became keeper of the Ohtas, the Delaware dolls. I never saw her dolls, because Grandma didn't want me, or anyone else of our generation, to see them. My mama did see them, daily; the two women lived with the Ohtas as if they were family, honoring them with special attentions, caring for them as if they were children. Grandma, especially, took her responsibility to the Delaware dolls as seriously as she took anything in her life.

One doll was a man, one a woman. Both were ancient and fragile. Sticks projected from beneath their clothes so they could be carried and held high during ceremonies. It was Grandma's job to keep them in excellent repair and to make new clothes for them before the Doll Dance, which took place each spring.

She sewed their new clothes from calico, using the thick steel needle that was a prized possession. She strung shell beads to hang round their necks, like tiny wampum strings. She patched and painted and sewed in new horsehair to keep those dolls in tip-top shape.

The dolls were old—older than Grandma—but they were often renewed. I don't know who made them first or how long ago. I know they were passed, mother to daughter, sister to sister, through a long line of Delaware women of the Turtle clan. I know also that, in the decades Grandma cared for them, she must have remade them top to toe, so that every scrap of cloth was hers, every stitch, every touch of color. I've made dolls myself, so I say this with some confidence: when Grandma patched and stitched and painted the dolls, she remade them according to her own idea of what they should be.

I'm not sure what the Ohtas and their dance meant to Grandma. Caring for them was a debt of honor she owed the tribe, an affirmation of all she valued, all she held sacred. As Keeper of the Dolls, it was Grandma's duty to host the Doll Dance. She prepared a feast to lay out on the long plank tables—hominy and corn soup, greens, jerked venison, wild turkey, fried corn bread. The dolls were feasted and feted; they were carried through the swirl of color and noise on the shoulders of the head dancers.

The season was spring, the dolls were man and woman, so the dance may have had something to do with the crop going into the ground, with fertility. Indians and fertility. We Delawares celebrated fertility in dance and song. And our numbers got smaller. The white folks didn't do any dances or ceremonies; they just multiplied. Go figure.

Some of the talk I've heard is that the Doll Dance was really about health more than about good harvests and birthing babies. Wellness and fertility . . . two sides of a coin, really, when it comes to the survival of the people. Grandma was a healer; many people relied on her medicines and cures. So the idea that the dolls had something to do with keeping the people healthy is satisfying in those personal terms.

In 1830 the Delawares, and Grandma with them, walked into the cauldron of pro- and antislavery warfare that was Kansas Territory. Surely the dolls protected us on that difficult trip, in that perilous place.

The reserved land in Kansas flowed with clear streams; the rich soil supported an abundant harvest of corn, beans, potatoes, melons, oats, and wheat. Game was plentiful, the Plains with their great herds were nearby. Some Delawares adopted the frame homes, the fences and plows, and the religion of white America. Charles Journeycake, Baptist preacher and respected council member, was a head of this modernist faction. Our politics began to change. Tribal leadership had always followed our division into three bands—Turkey, Turtle, and Wolf. Chief Journeycake should have been a Turkey; that was the vacancy he filled. Instead, he was the favorite of the Indian agent. For the first time, that was the more important consideration. Ten years later, we gave up our traditional leadership altogether.

Others, perhaps the majority, continued to live in the one-room cabins that had been our homes for a hundred years. These so-called traditionals still spoke only Delaware, broke the ground with digging sticks, trapped and hunted out on the Plains, relied on trade in pelts and hides as well as the annual distributions of treaty funds, and followed the traditional ceremonies of the Big House. Grandma Wahoney surely was one of the traditionals. She grew wise in the uses of herbs and began to earn her reputation as a healer.

I can't say for certain where they were born, but Grandma's children grew up in Kansas. I'm aware of two only—her daughter

Akweapailu, known by name alone, and a son known not even by name, but only by the story of his tragic death in Oklahoma. There may have been others—likely there were; it was a time when dying was the common fate of children—but they were never spoken of.

Kansas was home for thirty-eight years. We survived the battles over slavery. We sent 170 of our men to fight for the Union in the Civil War. After all that, it was the railroads that forced us out of Kansas. The settlers who came on the iron horse pressed us all around, and the Missouri River Railroad plagued us with demands to sell our land.

A delegation of our leading men went to the Cherokee Nation, south of Kansas in Indian Territory, to find a new tribal home. We bought the right to live on 157,000 acres of Cherokee land, centered on the Caney and Verdigris Rivers in what is now northeastern Oklahoma—the country I've lived in all my life. In 1868 Grandma set out on the last of her long walks. It must have been the hardest; physically, I'm sure it was. She was sixty-seven, a difficult time of life to pull up stakes and start over. She'd lived long in Kansas and must have thought of it as home. She could hardly know that she had forty years of living ahead of her in Oklahoma.

Once in Indian Territory, the Delawares actually purchased citizenship in the Cherokee Nation. We gave up our own tribal government and voted in Cherokee elections. To make up that loss, the people returned to some of the old ways with a new passion. The traditionals built a new Big House and held the twelve-day ceremony each year. The women revived the art of basketmaking and nearly forgotten recipes. They relied once again on the healing powers of medicinal herbs. Grandma Wahoney, now a revered elder and a noted healer, must have played a leading role in the revival.

The one story that does stand clear from the mists of this time before memory is the murder of Grandma's only son. It happened shortly after the Delaware trek into Indian Territory. The young man, who must have been a child of her later years, was hunting at the foot of the Osage Hills, in land still claimed by the old enemies of the Delawares dating back to their stay in Missouri. An Osage hunting party surprised the youth and killed him, placing crossed arrows on his body as a warning to other Delaware hunters. There was a memory of bloodshed between the tribes and a shared desire to avoid any renewal. Leading men met to discuss how to stop the shedding of more blood.

They decided that instead of fighting, the Osages and Delawares would meet each year to have a good time. One year the meeting would be in Osage country, the next in Delaware country. At each meeting, the Delawares would bring the food and the Osages would answer with presents intended to make up for the harm they'd done Grandma in killing her only son. As part of the festivities, tobacco was smoked until fragrant clouds rose above the campgrounds. For that reason the gatherings were known as "smokes."

It is not recorded just what role Ma Wah Taise played in arranging for these annual "smokes" that did so much to preserve the peace between Delawares and Osages. But as the principal injured party and a person of respect in her tribe, she must have given her assent to the arrangement. That idea is certainly consistent with what I know of her wisdom and generosity. That the "smokes" in Delaware country were held up on Post Oak Creek, north of the current town of Dewey—not too far from where Grandma and Phoebe lived in their one-room log cabin—lends credence to the notion that Grandma was a sort of hostess to the Delaware-Osage "smokes." Imagine the grace it must have taken to entertain the murderers of your only son in order to maintain the peace. Contrast that with our own blood lust in matters of crime.

Grandma Wahoney must have been somewhat over ninety when she stepped into my personal circle of memory. The galloping consumption, as it was called then, laid its bony hand on my grandma, Lisey Whiteturkey, and breathed its cold breath into her young nostrils. A virulent form of tuberculosis it may have been, or perhaps pneumonia. Grandma's herbal nostrums had no power against it, though she did battle with all the strength and cunning she possessed. Here is the mirror in which we glimpse the terror the disease inspired: my grandmother died under a tent on the east side of the house, where the prevailing winds would not blow her sickness back onto her family. Little Phoebe, innocent and unknowing, watched her mother die from the sanctuary of the big porch. The precautions were effective; the family escaped the ravages of plague.

Whether or not Sam bought Grandma's story that she might soon need Phoebe's help, he gratefully accepted her offer to raise one of his young children. Grandma moved Phoebe out before the women had a suitable house of their own. They went to live for a time with old lady Blackwing. The little girl was sung to sleep by the snoring of the two ancient women. The comfortable whine and rasp of their duet filled the cabin, leaving no room for night sounds—the howl of coyotes and whoo of owls—that could trouble a baby's sleep. Sometimes the din seemed to shake the cabin. Shadows on the wall danced to the terrific noise. Old lady Blackwing hung strips of drying pumpkin from her rafters; they looked like a crowd of puppets in the moonlight that drifted with its silver shadows through the smokehole in her roof. My mama, little Phoebe, would snuggle into her mattress of corn shucks and watch the host of shadows dance on the walls to the gentle ebb and flow of wind seeping through cracks in the walls. It was a wonderfully comfortable feeling.

There were other shadows on the wall at old lady Blackwing's place. Grandma Wahoney, as a Keeper of the Delaware Dolls, treated her Ohtas like members of her family. She kept them in her cabin, in a place of honor, where they could see and hear everything that happened, but where they couldn't get hurt. Sometimes she seemed to talk to them.

In old lady Blackwing's fine house, the dolls literally hung from the rafters. They stood about as tall as a forearm, elbow to finger's end. At night, depending on the angle of moonlight, their shadows could stretch to human length. They loomed large among the crowd of nervous dancers on the wall. To little Phoebe those giant shadows looked like the spirits she'd heard tell about, the Manitou of Grandma's stories, towering over skinny little people.

Grandma and Phoebe didn't live with old lady Blackwing any longer than necessary. Grandma had Sam Whiteturkey sell the 160-acre allotment that had belonged to her granddaughter Lisey, his recently dead wife. Settlers were starting to move into the area around Dewey and Bartlesville, and the allotment land was bringing in a pretty penny. Sam got enough from the sale of Lisey's acres to build himself and his three remaining children a fine frame house. Enough also to put up the traditional one-room cabin Grandma preferred along Coon Creek east of Dewey. Now Grandma and Phoebe had their own place.

The girl and the old woman spent much of their time alone together. They spoke Delaware. For my mother, English was the language of school, the language of the town; Delaware was the language of home and heart.

They planted a garden together, dropping each corn kernel and bean and pumpkin seed into a neat little hole made the old way, with a digging stick. They fertilized with dried minnows seined from Coon Creek. Mama could always coax a crop from Mother Earth; that knowledge was one of Grandma's legacies. For Ma Wah Taise, the woods were the great garden; she went out into the silent, shadowy pharmacy and harvested the bark and roots and fungus and herbs that she dried and mixed and brewed into her healing potions. She did not share her knowledge of medicine with Mama. The healing arts were certainly not for girls, and the reputation of healer was a burden she would not willingly pass on to the little one she so loved.

Sick people—Delawares and, increasingly, white settlers—came to Grandma's cabin looking for cures. It was a land of flooded bottoms in the spring and fierce heat in summer, of agues and plagues, of swarming mosquitoes, of cholera and malaria. Grandma claimed no shaman power, though there were some who gave her such credit, only the wisdom of the healing herbs learned in a long life.

The sick—and the well—traveled the muddy road that ran along Coon Creek, linking the new towns of Bartlesville and Dewey with the old Delaware homesteads and the small white settlements in the Scudder district, farther up along the creek. Mama's little sister Mamie was a frequent visitor at Grandma's cabin in summertime. In the stifling summer heat, Phoebe and Mamie would swim and splash in the slow, muddy waters of Coon Creek. They got to know the locals who made the long trek to town and back on all the errands that had become so necessary to life.

The Reeves, hardy white settlers with strong, strapping sons, were one family that regularly made the trip to town. Amos Reeve was quite a bit older than the Whiteturkey sisters—six years older than Phoebe—and he'd tease the pretty Delaware girls when he saw them cooling in the creek. His banter, as well as his handsome face and muscular physique, made a lasting impression on little Phoebe. What's more, Amos was training himself to be a rodeo cowboy, and sometimes he'd show off his new riding stunts. While still a girl, though clearly a girl in touch with the woman she would become, Phoebe told Mamie, "You know, that Amos Reeve is the best-looking one of the lot. Clever, too. I think I'm gonna marry that man." I'm not sure if it was the trick riding or something Amos said that captivated her so, but whatever it was, I'm grateful to it. It was momentous in my life, to say the least.

I think this is the right place to give away one of Grandma's little secrets. Under her long dress, in all weather, she invariably wore leather leggings. The leggings had a pocket; in that pocket she hid a tobacco pouch and a stubby clay pipe. Phoebe must have told the secret; later, when Amos came a courting, he always brought Grandma a gift of tobacco. The old lady accepted gratefully and put no obstacles in his path.

In late summer, Phoebe and Mamie tended their garden, put the cabin in order, helped load up their wagon, and set off with Ma Wah Taise for the Gamwing, the Big House ceremony that was the centerpiece of the Delaware religion. The Big House stood on high ground between the forks of Caney River, some miles from Grandma's cabin. It was a windowless rectangle constructed of unpainted logs and planks enclosing a dirt floor large enough to hold a crowd. Its most remarkable feature was the ancient faces carved on the center post and the interior posts, facing in each of the four directions. Grandma and her two little charges camped out, along with hundreds of other traditionals, for the few days it took to prepare the Big House, the twelve days when the fire burned continuously, and the thirteenth day, when the women were allowed to tell their stories.

Every participant had a job to do. Phoebe and Mamie got to help scour the hard-packed dirt floor and then spread a thick layer of clean straw where the grown-ups would sit during the chants and dances. Grandma was busy with the cooking. She also had to purify her body at a sweat, ready her traditional dress and strings of shell beads, and braid her thinning white hair—all in preparation for her very special role in the Big House.

A feature of the ceremony was the recitation of Delaware history, beginning with the creation story and running through the treaties and tribal wanderings remembered with the aid of precious strings and belts of wampum. Some of the Big House legends were more personal—encounters of living people with the forces of the universe we call Manitou. Ma Wah Taise chanted at the Big House ceremony. She had the honor of being first to perform at the Atehumwin, the ritual of the thirteenth day, after the fire was allowed to burn out. The dignified old woman, dressed in her finest, took the turtle-shell rattle from the leader, moved into the inner circle, and began to dance the slow shuffle of the women around the white path. Her song recounted the magical adventure of her childhood—her rescue by Otter Woman and Tiny Man Woodpecker—as I have told it.

Phoebe and Mamie were not permitted inside the Big House; they played outside with the other children while the adults prayed, sang, and danced. At dusk, an old devil wearing a bearskin might emerge from the shadowy woods to tease and terrify the children. Grandma made sure her girls were well supplied with tobacco to offer the demonic figure so he would leave them in peace. It wasn't until Phoebe noticed a shirt collar under the bearskin that she realized the wolf man was an actor playing a part.

Grandma Wahoney was considered by many in the tribe to be a seer. Her visions were not momentous; they were simply a part of her life. Once, for example, she called Phoebe and Mamie in from their play. "There's a mad dog about," she said, and ordered the girls into the cabin. Grandma stood on her chair, ax in hand, and awaited the dog's arrival. In time it staggered into the yard, foaming and snarling. The old lady calmly struck it dead with her ax. Another time, Phoebe was out playing with her little dog named Hey Hey. Both of them, for their different reasons, were digging about in the riverbank when they dislodged a heavy rock that cracked Hey Hey in the head. The little dog went limp; to all appearances, Hey Hey was dead. Phoebe ran back to the cabin, begging Grandma to help her bring back the poor lifeless pet. Grandma shook her head. "Hey Hey isn't dead. She'll be all right, just give her a little time." And sure enough, the next morning, her head swollen from the blow, Hey Hey staggered back to the cabin, where she soon recovered. Those were instances of Grandma's uncanny foresight that my mother encountered in the course of her growing up.

In the last year of her life, the character of Grandma Wahoney's prophetic visions changed. Otter Woman appeared to her and told her to make herself ready. Grandma was 107 years old at the time, although still able to carry in her firewood, so the supernatural warning came as no great surprise. Grandma told Phoebe, "I'll be leaving you soon, but have no fear. It will be as easy as falling asleep, and then I'll go to a happy place."

Grandma thought about the world she would leave behind and saw that it was changing rapidly. One day, walking with Phoebe, she looked up to see a large hawk circling in the sky. She held the girl's hand hard and said, "Someday you'll see something in the sky that looks like a hawk. But it will be much bigger than a hawk and fly far higher. It will have men in it." The girl looked at the old woman as if she was touched in the head. Neither of them knew anything about the possibility of airplanes.

Grandma valued Delaware tradition above all else. In her life and her person, she was Delaware tradition. And yet she understood that the time for her way of living would pass with her passing. The world had changed, and the past could prove a burden.

The old lady could not simply go off into her good night. First she had to solve the problem of the Delaware dolls. They were her responsibility to the end. In a sense they represented the power of the Turtle Delaware women: the power to nurture, the power to heal. She could do with them only what tradition allowed. The dolls were an inheritance, and Grandma had outlived most of the women who were entitled to receive them. Only her great-granddaughters, Phoebe and Mamie, remained in that line.

There's a mystery to the action she took. I'll never fully understand; we're from different worlds, after all. I am old enough, though, to grasp the notion that the world can become unrecognizable. I know Grandma saw the traditionals growing old and dying, saw the young people turn away from the Big House, turn toward Christianity, toward the white man's dress and schooling. She saw the ceremonies that sustained her wither. She came to despair for the future of her Delaware people.

Grandma decided that she would not burden her beloved Phoebe with the care of the dolls. Phoebe was a married woman now, with a new baby. Her life would be lived in a future very different from anything Grandma had known. Ma Wah Taise would be the last Keeper of the Delaware Dolls. The precious dolls that she had tended with such love for so many years would die with her. She stipulated in her will that they should be buried with her in her grave. "The dolls are too big a responsibility," she told Phoebe. "In a few years, no one will care. Only you. And that will break your heart. They should come with me when I go to a better place."

Indian Territory became the state of Oklahoma in 1907. Grandma Wahoney passed from this world peacefully, as she predicted, in 1908. It happened this way: Grandma was entertaining company, sitting on her bed in the midst of friends, when she put back her head to laugh. The breath of life left her with her laugh. She was buried in the old Delaware cemetery, along with her dolls, in a traditional ceremony; a hand-carved wooden cross was placed at her head. Her action ended the Doll Dance she'd hosted for so many decades. Big House ceremonies continued for another twenty years, but the old religion withered as its practitioners died. Grandma's century ended, effectively, with her death. In a few years, mine began.

Ma Wah Taise was a Turtle Delaware; so is Pima Pen Okwe. Clan membership is one of her legacies. There are others. More than she could have imagined; more than I understood until I became an old woman myself. The dolls I never saw have whispered and cajoled at the edge of consciousness all my life and emerged as a powerful influence in my later years. The marvelous old woman I never met became one of the bright, fixed stars in my night sky very early on. One of the themes of my book will be the powerful influence that the Keeper of the Delaware Dolls has had on my life.

Four

BACK HOME
AGAIN

It's not the going home that's especially hard; it's the sights that await when you get there. When the world spins around enough times, it changes utterly. That's especially true when the place you're visiting is vivid in your mind, where it lives as a memory of paradise. Come along with me for a look at my home place, and you'll see what I mean.

Leslie, my sister Betty's boy, owns Mama's old allotment now. Leslie's an interesting fellow, worth spending some time with. He's a weekend rodeo cowboy, a bronc rider with some fine, wide, hand-tooled leather belts proclaiming his success in big-time Oklahoma rodeos. He has about the dandiest cowboy boots—just fancy enough, if you know what I mean—all the tooling softened and dyed by dust. Weekdays, Leslie's a lawyer. He has done the legal work for our Delaware tribe. Maybe he's the only Delaware who's passed the bar, I don't know. I do know he's the only Delaware lawyer with a sweat lodge on his place.

So you see, Leslie can play cowboy and Indian without help. And then settle the argument in court. I don't believe he does that; all I mean to say is that with the changes going on, some people live pretty complicated lives. Leslie was a cowboy before he was much of an Indian, which might surprise you. But then,

Oklahoma was cowboy country before it turned back to promoting itself as Indian Territory a decade or so ago.

Leslie's place is about three and a half miles due east of Dewey, near Coon Creek, a site of Delaware and Cherokee settlement a century ago. He isn't home today; it's a summer Saturday and his little girl is signed up for a local barrel race. So we'll have to put off that talk. He knows we're coming, and he's given us leave to explore the home place at our leisure.

We have to walk through a neighbor's pasture before we get to the woods that run down to the creek. I guess somewhere along the way a chunk of the acreage was sold off; I don't remember. We follow one of those old, rutted wagon tracks the well riggers used back when big and little grasshopper pumps pulled oil and natural gas out of just about every parcel of land in this part of the state. The pump is still now, choked with rust, a reminder of the time when black gold—and not, as in the *Wizard of Oz*, yellow brick—paved the road from farm to city.

The woods are quiet; people don't live in them as they did when I was a kid. They don't look familiar. The trees we climbed are bigger now, or dead. The underbrush is thick and tangled in many places. I think there was an order in the woods when we lived here that's missing now. I don't see the thickets of huckleberries and raspberries, the grapevines and wild plums that were such delicious additions to our morning meal. I don't see the clusters of wildflowers that my sisters and I used to gather and arrange in the porcelain vases that were my mother's pride. Maybe my old eyes aren't sharp enough; perhaps I'm in too much of a hurry to see clearly. I haven't been to the home place in quite a while.

We come upon a clearing where some trees were cut years ago. Tree fungus fringes the stumps like overstarched shirt collars. A thick black snake maybe six feet long—a racer I think—suns itself on one of the rotten stumps. The heat has made it sleepy. I'm not surprised to see it. We had snakes eighty years ago; we have them on my farm now. Rattlers, cottonmouths, water moccasins—we treat them with plenty of respect. Racers, king snakes, hog snakes—those we pretty much ignore. So we don't give this one a wide berth, and when we get close it untangles itself and grudgingly slithers off the stump and out of sight.

Soon we're there. No wall stands; there's no reminder of home aboveground. I recognize the spot only from the old cellar, still sunk a couple of feet. No stick from the house remains, no rotting board. The only telltale sign of life gone by is this—when you run your hands through the dirt where I guess the kitchen was, you find shards of pottery, hundreds of them, little timeworn fragments of flower-pattern blue china. I don't know why we left it there, I vaguely remember the blue as Mama's favorite set. But there's no arguing with the facts; some dedicated archaeologist could probably piece together the better part of three or four place settings if he had a mind to.

Two limestone slabs stand some little way beyond; a third lies fallen, crusted by moss and lichen, nearly buried itself. I remember they're grave markers, though I've forgotten, if I ever knew, whose resting places they mark. Time has wiped away any trace of whatever message ushered the departed into the hereafter. If the dead were Delawares, as I suppose they were, they would have been buried with the wooden markers that still stand here and there in our tribal cemetery. But no trace of those remains. Who will recognize them as tombstones, or honor the dead with so much as a quizzical look, when I am gone?

The cellar seems no bigger than a room, two rooms tops, yet in my memory it was a spacious house. Trees—big trees, oak and pecan and mimosa—have grown up within the walls. And yet I lived in the space they occupy. How can enough time have passed for the habitations of my youth to have sunk so completely back into the forest?

But that's what has happened. On the banks of Coon Creek, the cabin where my big sister Indie was born has vanished. The wagon road that once tied Bartlesville to the allotments stretching east has left no trace on the heavy scrub that borders the creek today. The creek itself is sluggish and brackish; it's lost all joy in its movement. We swam in the creek when I was a girl, and drank its brown water when the summer sun parched us, without thought or fear or consequence. I would not drink it today, I promise you.

Three-quarters of a mile farther east on that road was the cabin where Grandma Wahoney raised Mama. We could walk almost all the way to it on our own land, and the neighbors made no objection when we crossed their place, even if we helped ourselves to a peach or some pecans in season. You'd never know when you passed Grandma's cabin now. I might be able to spot something; I knew the place so very well once. I'm not sure, though; time has worked its changes.

The Coon Creek settlement is gone, unremembered, less than history unless I can restore it. I do remember. I especially re-member the neighbors with kids. We lived in the old Delaware Purchase. Most of our neighbors were Delawares, like the Long-bones, whose place was just above ours, whose kids were our pals and playmates. But there were others, neighbors, friends, who lived comfortably among us. The Wittenburgs, just down the road, were Cherokees. We'd visit their place, they'd come see us. Sometimes they'd sit down at our table and then spend the night. Papa didn't let us do overnights, so I guess the eighty-year-old Wittenburg kids still owe me a few sleepovers.

Just a little past Grandma's place and then south a ways you'd find the Test. The Test was an oil camp; the men who dug the wells and tended the pumps that sent oil and natural gas coursing through pipelines to heat and drive a nation lived there, sometimes with their families. It was a small city of frame houses, outhouses, a water well with pumps, a big central storm cellar. It must have been rough living for the children, but they got through it. The Coonfields lived in the Test; they were white, but rough and ready just like the rest of us.

School was about a mile from our place. We walked to it in all sorts of weather, as did all the others. In the long planting and harvesting summer, we kids were pretty much on our own. We'd meet at the swimming holes during the day, make the summer circuit in the evenings. We'd pile up great bonfires and tell all sorts of stories in the garish light of dancing flames—the Longbone kids, the Wittenburg kids, the Coonfield kids, the Reeve kids, and others.

Folks have moved on to other locales; the woods claim the Coon Creek settlement now. The same can be said for the prosperous Delaware homesteads, with their two-story frame houses, on the forks of the Caney River. Little Hogshooter Creek has shrunk to a trickle; even Captain Curleyhead's big stone root cellar, which stood proudly on its banks for decades, has tumbled back into the dirt. Remains of the thriving community on the Verdigris are drowned under fifty feet of water. I may be the only one who can recognize vestiges of some of the sites we've just visited—humble stages for much of the drama in this book.

Rivers are no longer the arteries of travel and commerce, the veins on the leaf of settlement. The insurance companies discourage home building on the floodplains, and this is an age of insurance. I don't argue; I have insurance myself. My house stands on high ground. But there was something grand about the spirit that accepted the risk of flood in return for the gift of flood, which was food on the table—and lived life on those uncompromising terms.

Ah, the memories . . . they come pouring back as I stand in the depression that was once our cellar. I bend down to dig up a couple of pottery shards. I want to take them back with me; I'll hold them when I return to my own place, so I can remember it all. I think they're like the seeds that grew Jack's beanstalk; they have the power to take me to a land of fond memory. And while I'm talking to you, that's precisely where I want to live.

A Memory
of Paradise

Five

TOUCHED BY
THE DELAWARE

The Reeve family lived in the heart of the old Delaware Purchase —the land our wandering tribe bought a half century before from the Cherokee Nation. Then came the Sooner land rush, statehood, the Dawes Act. The government split up the big tribal holdings into allotments and sold off the rest. We found ourselves neighbored mostly by Delaware families, living on their parcels of land. Cherokees were scattered about; Osage country bordered ours on the West. White settlers were buying up the Indian allotments when they could and moving into northeastern Oklahoma.

Let me take you back to my home place, where I grew up for sixteen years. I think that's the best way to give you a feel for the life that was lived in native and pioneer settlements seventy years ago.

At first my folks made their home in a rough-hewn log cabin Papa built on the banks of Coon Creek. My sister Indie was born there; Grandma Wahoney visited and blessed the baby before she died. It was a tiny place. Papa talked Mama into selling off ten acres of her allotment and ordered up the big two-story frame that was my childhood home. The exterior was unpainted, weathered wood. We had four finished rooms on the first floor—bedroom, living room, dining room, and kitchen. Some of the furniture was good period stuff, Victorian style with ornate carving. I remember two upholstered chairs at the ends of our dining table with arms and feet like that. But the table itself, and the chairs for us kids, was fashioned from planks by one of our local woodworkers. Big black cast-iron pots and skillets hung from pegs on the kitchen wall. We had a wood stove, of course, and something that may surprise you.

Our pride and joy was a gas stove that provided more even heat than wood. How can that be? Well, it so happened that we had small oil and natural gas wells on the place. Mama leased her mineral rights to the Indian Territory Illuminating Oil Company, a forerunner of City Service. It was an event when the royalty money came in every couple of months; we'd pile into the wagon and head to town to load up on supplies. But back to the stove, which ran on natural gas pumped right on our spread. We didn't have enough to sell, but Papa ran a pipeline in from the well so Mama could enjoy the very up-to-date advantages of cooking with gas. She really was a good cook; maybe the pride she felt when she turned the knob and put a match to the gas jet inspired her.

We had two stoves downstairs, but in the cavernous upstairs we relied on body heat. The big room, divided only by the stairway, was furnished with two iron beds, king size beds to say the least. The girls slept on one, the boys on the other. The walls were raw timber; when the north wind blew, it whistled through cracks between the boards. We knew when it snowed overnight; we'd wake up to find a white blanket laid neatly over the floor and our bedclothes. Even so, we kept toasty warm under a great heap of quilts. I was the youngest girl for years and slept in the middle, embraced by sisters on either side and nearly smothered under a pile of thick feather quilts. On frigid nights, my sisters would heat up an iron or a brick, wrap it up in blankets, and set it at the foot of the bed. I didn't really need to do that; I always slept warm.

All sorts of necessities hung from our rafters, especially in winter. Hams and some big catfish that Papa cured in our smokehouse. Pelts from the rabbits and squirrels and coons and skunks that my brother Henry caught in his trapline and sold for a good price over in Dewey. Strings of onions and turnips and wild roots. Grandma Wahoney's dolls never made their way to our rafters; they were buried with her before I was born. But Mama did have two wampum belts hanging in a place of honor. They were a couple of inches wide, two, two and a half feet long. I remember an intricate pattern of black on white shells. I don't know what happened to Mama's wampum; I suspect she may have sold the belts to buy us school shoes. I'm sure I enjoyed the shoes at the time, but now, with twenty-twenty hindsight, I really do wish that she'd hung on to those belts of beads.

Mama kept two gardens, and of course we girls helped. Directly west of the house we had a stand of corn and a potato patch. In late summer you could walk right out the door, dig up some potatoes and pick a few ears of corn, then fry it all up for breakfast. That was a delicious meal. A short walk north was a bigger field, where Mama planted peas and beans, onions, tomatoes, beets, carrots. I think Grandma taught Mama all the Delaware tricks with growing things. She had a famous garden, and as busy as we were canning and putting up jams, there was always plenty to trade with neighbors or just give away to those who were less fortunate.

Delaware, Cherokee, white, Osage, it didn't much matter to us. We pretty much accepted our neighbors as folks, even did a lot of intermarrying. We never thought, this thing we're doing now is Delaware. Grandma Wahoney and even generations before her did pretty much the same. Planted corn, seined minnows, dug roots for eating, smoked tobacco, things like that. We lived a life that seemed natural to us and never considered what might be native and what European, any more than we made that distinction about the plants that grew in our woods and fields. The woods looked fine, our life felt right; that was all I needed to know then.

Now, when I've been asked the question a goodly number of times and thought about my life in those terms, I can point to some of the things we did that were touched by Delaware tradition. I want to talk about that side of my life, so long as you realize that we didn't treat it special, or understand it to be more important. Often the Delaware was fun, and we were happy to recognize that.

That was especially true of Saturday nights in summer, which were highlights of our social calendar. You really got an idea of the number of Delawares who lived within a good walk or wagon ride of each other come Saturday night. Just about all the Delawares in our part of the country, plenty of Cherokees, white friends too, made their Saturday way to Jim Jackson's spread, two, three miles north of our home place. You'd hear a lot of Delaware talked by the old ones—I think that's why Mama liked so much to come. But hardly any kids my age knew how to speak the old language, or cared to know.

During the day the Jacksons held a rousing game of Indian football on their grounds. At sunset they lit great bonfires and put on a stomp dance. Let me explain these two delightful social institutions in a little more detail.

Indian football was played with much enthusiasm and few rules. The ball was about half the size of a basketball, made of deerhide and stuffed with deer hair. It was approximately round and definitely hard. The playing field was irregularly shaped, with protected goals on either end; if there was an out-of-bounds, it seldom came up during the play. The teams pitted men against the women. The older women all wore aprons so they could carry the ball wrapped up in them. The women could throw and catch, do just about anything to advance toward the goal. The men could move the ball only by kicking.

But if there were rules about what you could do with the ball, I'm not aware of any governing contact with other persons. Any number could play, and the game was open to anyone who wanted; when Mama and her girls played, Papa and his boys did too. So the sides were large and the field was crowded. Men and women pushed and shoved, tripped, kicked, pulled hair, laughed, flirted, agreed to partner in the evening dance, came to blows. Anyone from old to young could play, so I was coaxed or pushed out onto the playing field from time to time. I was considered something of a baby, though, a little girl who hid behind her mother's skirts and cried a bit too easily. In my defense, I was one of the youngest girls out on the football field, and little girls were at the bottom of the pecking order. There was reason to be afraid, and I'm not ashamed of my sissy behavior. Anyway, I outgrew it.

The stomp dance began in the evening—often after football. The footballers would change into fresh clothes, take an hour to eat and recharge, then dance far into the night. The sheer stamina required was prodigious, but those old-time Indians were a hearty lot. The dance ground was sun-baked dirt and grass compacted into a kind of concrete by stomping feet. It was hard, especially in the moccasins most of the dancers wore. Men and women circled round and round the drum. The pop of resinous logs in the great bonfires added a savage note to the rhythmic beat of drummers and stompers; shadow dancers stretched out in weird postures on the orange-tinted ground.

Men beat the drum; women shook rattles tied to their legs to create a sound like waves crashing on a distant but well-remembered shore. It was the women who gave the stomp dance its name. Certain of our women had the right to tie rattles to their legs and shake out a dance rhythm by stomping their feet into the ground. In ceremonial dances, those rattles were hollow turtle shells. But the Saturday evening stomps at Jim Jackson's place were purely social affairs. The rattles were improvisations, mostly made from condensed-milk cans filled with pebbles. The women would lace about half a dozen of those cans up their legs and circle the dance grounds, shaking and stomping up a storm. It took strength and considerable skill to do it. I'm afraid I thought they looked kind of silly with all those cans tied on. The turtle rattles made a much better appearance, but I suppose the tin cans did the job. They made noise. And what a glorious noise it was. In the right mood, in the right light, I can close my eyes now and hear the faintest echo of drum and rattle, laughter and song in the empty silence that possesses what was once Jim Jackson's stomp dance ground.

Jim Jackson's place was Delaware country, no doubt about it; the stomp dance echoed through centuries. The Delaware wasn't always that clear, though; sometimes I only caught a glimpse of it years later, looking back, and never suspected at the time.

When my little sister Betty and I began to make our mud dolls, I never saw Grandma Wahoney lurking just out of sight in the tall weeds of the riverbank, smiling at our play. I knew Grandma had been Keeper of the Dolls, but I never made a connection between what we were doing and her Delaware dolls, so important to the women in my line for centuries. Now, looking back, I see more connections than I ever would have guessed at when I was doing the living instead of the looking.

You see, we had a natural clay deposit, a treasure open to all, on one of the steep banks of Coon Creek. This was pure clay; you could have fired it with fine results if there was a need. After the spring floods had receded and the creek returned to a level that made the banks safe, Betty and I would hurry down, dig our hands up to the elbow in the yielding clay, and pull out hefty chunks. We hauled our treasure back to a sheltered spot, where we hoped heavy rain wouldn't penetrate, and began to build the props that would last the long summer season.

At first, when we were babies, we made clumsy little figures. We called them our little bears, and they probably did look as much like bears as people. They stood erect and had recognizable arms and legs, but their faces had the small eyes, rounded ears, and long snouts of teddy bear faces. We each made ourselves a bear family and let the figures dry until they were hard enough to stand up to rough handling. Then we played out all sorts of stories; not bear stories at all, but real family stories of summer adventures, days in school and church, trips to town—all the things that added excitement and variety to our lives.

The primitive bear stage didn't last long. The whole point of making our own clay dolls was that we could create all the actors and props we needed to put on what really were little plays. In just a few summers our games became elaborate, absorbing affairs. We made ourselves houses, three, four feet long, with sturdy adobe outside walls and thinner walls dividing the rooms. We fashioned tables and chairs, beds, lamps, pots and pans, dinner plates, tiny little glasses. Believe me, we labored with all the care we could muster to make sure our houses were furnished to the best possible standard.

When all the props were ready, we set to work on the families that would live in our respective homes for a full season. We still called them bears, but we made them look as much like people as we could. Like the Creator, we fashioned generations of men and women from the mud. I would begin with an old grandma in all her wrinkled dignity and work my way down to plump, bawling babies. Our creations didn't come alive, except in our imaginations, but they sure did get hard. We set them out to bake under the hot sun, and in a few days they were so rocklike that it took prolonged exposure to water to soften them up. Storm rescue became an obligation. Threatening clouds sent Betty and me racing out to our houses, tarps in hand, to protect what was ours from destruction.

We both got to be good at modeling. I mean, the faces could be pretty, handsome, have character. Of course mine were better made; I was, after all, five years older. But Betty always insisted that her furnishings were grander, her people lovelier and more lifelike. She was a competitive one, was Betty, and she never gave me an inch.

I suppose that the people I fashioned out of river clay were, in truth, my earliest dollmaking efforts. They were very basic — the clothes, everything, sculpted out of mud. But some of them, as I think back on it, really were well done. There was nothing especially Indian about them, though some were Indians, as were so many of the people who lived around us. Although I knew all about Grandma Wahoney and the dolls she'd taken with her to the grave, I never made any connection between her role and my summer play. These weren't Delaware dolls, they were simply the fantasy playmates of a summer's day. And yet . . .

Jim Jackson's stomp dances and the bear families Betty and I dreamed up, perhaps with a little help from Grandma Wahoney, by no means exhausted the Delaware influence on my young life. But as I've told you, it was all a seamless whole. I'm not about to take a knife to my life, cut out the Delaware, and lay it before you here and now. Mostly we'll get to it when it comes up. But I do want to show, with just a few examples, that the native world didn't pass with Grandma's passing. Much of it colored what I like to think of as the rural paradise of my early years.

Six

I REMEMBER
MAMA

She stands in my memory this way: framed in the doorway of Saint Paul's Episcopal Church in Dewey, wearing her Sunday best—a navy blue dress with white polka dots, white collar, and brooch. It was a dress she sewed herself, as she made all our clothes. Her long, coarse black hair glistens in the sun. A touch of rouge awakens the copper in her cheeks; charcoal from a burnt match darkens her eyebrows and shadows her lids. She has no vanity, but she has regard for beauty, even her own. Her face is broad; prominent cheekbones frame her dark, penetrating eyes; her skin is smooth as a peach. She's a woman of average height, my height, but there's something commanding about her presence. Her figure is full, not supple anymore, but graceful and strong. Mama is a fine-looking woman; in all that congregation no one holds a candle to her.

Most of the Episcopalians at Saint Paul's were white, fair-skinned women unsuited to the sun. Our Oklahoma summers sucked the juice out of them, fried them and dried them. Mama, who was as much an outlander as any of the European women, had skin as smooth as beaten copper. She was a full-blood Delaware, her beauty perfectly suited to the ferocity of our summer sun. When I was a girl this part of the country had its share of full-bloods—handsome, dignified men and women with wise, serious eyes. You'd be hard pressed now to fill even a little room with full-blood Delawares.

Our family, along with Aunt Shirley and Uncle Joe, made up the full complement of Indians in the congregation. I don't know that Mama felt she was in a spotlight. I do know that she was careful to dress her four daughters in the latest styles, perfectly copied from the Sears catalog—the arbiter of fashion in our world. Phoebe Whiteturkey Reeve was a good Christian woman, kind and loving in all her ways, and she was respected in the church for her character. Even so, it was important to her to make certain no family painted a prettier, more up-to-date picture than her girls.

Church has been important to me all my life. The first church, Saint Paul's Episcopal, offered comforts of its own. It was a big, high-ceiling room of polished wood; the altar and the benches and the door lintels and ceiling rafters gleamed from constant rubbing. Reflected in the high-backed benches we could see the darling little hats Mama made us. They were pink georgette built on a frame of wire, but of course no hint of the wire showed. She crocheted flowers and sewed ribbons onto our hats; I felt wonderful just sitting and looking at mine, perched on my head and mirrored in the bright mahogany.

Another thing I remember about church is seeing my mama's hands folded in prayer. They were strong hands, work-worn, but they could be so gentle and looked graceful when she prayed. I think I'm struck by that because it may be the only time I ever saw her hands at rest. When she wasn't at church or asleep, Mama was perpetually at work.

Phoebe Whiteturkey Reeve was an accomplished woman. There was nothing a rural wife was called on to do that she didn't do well. But let's stop calling her Phoebe. That's the name on her grave marker, but it's not the name anyone called her.

Mama's Delaware name was Weetdolly, and family and friends called her Dolly. Aunt Dolly she was to all our little playmates. So, from here on it's Dolly Reeve who flashes us a smile as she hurries past, always busy with something.

They don't hand out gold medals for the things Dolly Reeve was good at. She didn't expect anything like that; I doubt she ever thought of herself that way. And yet I know it was important to her to do well the tasks of a woman as the white world reckoned them. I've told you already about our clothes. Mama made every stitch we wore, from rough-and-ready work clothes to dresses that were the pride of the countryside. She sewed our bonnets, our coats, our mittens, all.

Sewing was likely the first skill Dolly mastered; when she was fourteen, Grandpa Sam bought her a Singer sewing machine. The Singer was a proud thing—heavy steel, black with delicate little flowers painted on, that folded into a wooden case. Mama pumped the treadle as she nimbly pulled and turned the cloth. Singers were almost unbreakable; Mama used her machine to make . . . it must have been hundreds of things over the years. To own such a machine was an obligation. Tailors had them and almost no one else. Mama had to sew as well as a tailor, and she did. Without benefit of form or frame, she studied a picture, took her measurements, cut patterns out of newspaper, and worked her magic. I don't think there was anything she couldn't make.

Mama not only sewed our clothes, she washed them. Now, that was an entirely different proposition in those days than it is today. First she had to make the soap, a concoction of lye from wood ash mixed with rendered fat. She boiled the white things in a big galvanized tub, stirred the soap in with a thick ladle, took them down to the well to rinse. In summer we hung them up on the line, in winter the wet clothes dried around our fire. The colored things we took down to a big old washer by the well.

Mama, Indie, Ruth, and I would load up the tub, pour in soap and bluing. Henry would draw water from the well and heat it up with a torch. He'd sit atop the machine, working the agitator by hand. It took plenty of elbow grease to get those coloreds clean.

Most of what we ate we raised right on our place. Which is to say that Mama brought our food out of the ground. She planted two gardens, more than an acre in all of corn and potatoes, tomatoes, squash, beans, okra, beets, poke, onions. She put the seeds into the earth with a little prayer, a dusting of pollen, a dried fish in each pile of corn seeds. Then she pulled weeds, every day inspecting and digging out the unwanted greens and milkweed, thistles and wild flowers. We had an old scarecrow, very unconvincing I thought, and a dog on guard to run off the cottontails and other hungry critters. We didn't water the garden, couldn't, but relied on the rains—fierce and driving in the spring—and the rhythms of flood and drought. Coon Creek spilled over its banks during the spring rains to soak the soil that held the seed. It must not have happened often in late summer, though. I recall one time, when I was eight or so, when the flood began rising toward our ripening field. I guess I thought the water would rot our crop; I got all the baskets and buckets I could find and rushed out to pick beans. By the time the water reached my bare feet, I'd pretty well cleared the field of squash and tomatoes too. I felt enormously proud of having rescued the harvest, and Mama took me seriously enough to heap praise on my heroic efforts. Of course the flood would have done no harm, as I learned soon enough. I always thought of myself as being helpful, but I don't think I ever again worked quite so hard to bring in the crops for Mama.

Summertime, and the living was easy. The gardens provided. But summer ends, and much of Mama's work was in preparation for winter. She put up the fruits of the garden in jars and crocks and cans that filled and sagged the long wooden shelves of our pantry. Canning was hard, hot, sweaty work over black boiling kettles. The pleasure isn't in the doing; what pleasure there is comes four months later, when you open a can to find the contents savory and sweet.

Canning, I guess, is about as humble an occupation as you can imagine. Woman's work. But I remember reading about a Greek fellow who was considered a hero, for all that he performed some humble enough tasks. Cleaning out a stable, for one thing. I guess what made Hercules' labors heroic was that a man did them. Women have been doing pretty much the same thing day in, day out from the beginning.

Consider one instance out of many—the time Mama put up three entire beef cattle. This was during the depression; I was old enough to help but don't remember doing much helping. Cattle feed was scarce; cows were dying bony because the ranchers couldn't afford to feed them. The government decided to give away beefs to families who could butcher and use them. The Reeve family took three. We had mouths to feed, but there was no way we could eat our way through three cattle—about a half ton of meat—before the rot set in. So Mama had to can nearly all of that meat. What she did was to boil and grind the beef—I think the men did help with some of that grinding—and pack little patties, like baby hamburgers, in the rendered beef fat. She packed away a thousand pounds of meat in beef suet in what must have been hundreds of sealed glass jars. Papa had to build more shelves in the cellar to hold it all. Put up that way, the meat stayed fresh indefinitely. We had beef patties meal after meal and were glad to have them, though I may have voiced a complaint now and then about the monotony of our dinner fare.

I don't guess it occurred to me at the time that there was anything heroic about putting up three beefs; that was just the kind of thing Mama did. I was rather more impressed with feeding, collecting eggs, and cleaning up after four hundred chickens, along with an assortment of ducks, geese, turkeys, and the occasional guinea. You see, I had to help with that chore. I did feel just a bit like Hercules after sweeping out the henhouse and loading the coops with clean straw. The information that Grandma Wahoney had once made some sort of healing brew out of chicken guano didn't make me any more enthusiastic about the nasty chore. But it was Mama, not me, who so often emerged from the vast, dark, dank, suffocating array of coops, arms stained gray green, after eyedropping some home remedy down the gullets of the hens that had stopped laying or rescuing a new batch of chicks from suffocating in straw. A great crowd of squawking, squabbling chickens would follow her about the yard as she tossed feed from a big burlap sack around her neck. She would laugh at the tumult, though the birds sometimes scared me with the ferocity of their hunger; there was no doubt who was in charge of our fowl.

The point of all the planting and weeding and feeding, of course, was eating. We ate well, and some of our vast and varied diet, I'm convinced, came from the cookpots of Grandma Wahoney. We ate the fruit of the prickly pear, for instance, wiping off the stickers with an old rag, which we burned when it became so saturated with sweet juice and bristling with cactus spines that it was a dangerous temptation to dogs and small children. Mama showed us where to find a root we called Indian bread. I didn't know it then, but it looked like ginseng—white, and always with two little legs. When it was in season, in late summer, we'd dig it up, peel off the skin, and eat it raw. I remember it being chewy, with a hint of sweetness. I guess the prickly pear and Indian bread were our summer treats, our Twinkies and jelly rolls, not so sweet but probably a lot better for you.

Some of our exotic dishes required a good deal more preparation. I remember a kind of a stew we called pitukëna that Mama made from milkweed plants. She'd boil the plant, without the poisonous pods, for hours, then drain off the water, leaving behind a delicious white sauce. She'd prepare tiny little dumplings and boil them up in the sauce. Pitukëna had a wonderful fragrance and a delicate taste; it was a real treat.

Jackrabbits abounded in the tallgrass prairie that stretched out away from the river bottoms. Big eared, long legged, and very tasty. What we'd do was this: Papa would take the car out into the prairie and ride around to spook the rabbits. The big kids — Indie and Ruth and Henry and me sometimes — would ride out on the running board, stick in hand. When we'd see a big rabbit, we'd all jump off the running board and run him down. Then we'd club him with our sticks; that way you wouldn't ruin the hide with buckshot.

Mama would skin those rabbits and cook them up just about any way you could imagine — baked, boiled, fried, or mixed with the vegetables from the garden to make a stew. The dish I liked best was jackrabbit scrapple. What you'd do was to boil a whole rabbit until the meat was just about falling off the bones. Then you'd season some cornmeal, mix it up into mush, pack it around the pieces of rabbit, and let it all get hard. You'd drop those slices of mush and rabbit into hot lard and fry them up until they were golden brown and crispy. Boy, that was good. Jackrabbit scrapple; I haven't had it in sixty-five years. We just about killed off the jackrabbits in these parts, and that put an end to some mighty fine cooking.

We ate what the land provided. What the rivers and even the air provided, too. Sometimes Henry would snare little birds — pipers and partridges and meadowlarks and even blackbirds — and we'd eat those with relish. I remember one time we were lucky with blackbirds, and on a whim Papa decided we'd all eat like kings with blackbirds baked in a pie. Mama thought he was being silly, so he had Indie bake our blackbirds—just the little breasts, actually—into a pie. We each ate a piece, Mama too. I don't remember how it tasted, but I'm quite certain it was a dainty dish.

Cooking, cleaning, washing, mending, sewing, planting, harvesting, canning, gathering eggs, and on and on . . . the woman's work that kept Dolly Reeve's hands so busy that I only remember seeing them still at church, in prayer. But I don't want to give you the idea that her life, her accomplishment, was confined to the domestic. Mama was the daughter of a time and place that held Annie Oakley to be a model woman, and she could shoot a gun and ride a horse with the best of them. She'd sit Old Brownie just as pretty as a picture and put that horse through his paces. And Mama could shoot, pistol or rifle, with dead-eye accuracy. Papa used to say that his Dolly could shoot a jackrabbit from a galloping horse with a .38. I don't know if he ever saw her make that shot, I never did, but it shows the regard he held her in. He couldn't have made such a shot himself, I'm sure of that.

If a woman were her work and nothing more, my portrait of Phoebe Reeve would be complete. But a woman is always more than her work, even in frontier Oklahoma. I think that a woman is always her love first and foremost, and then, often, her mystery.

Mama's heart requires no validation from me. She was a Christian woman, by which I mean she possessed a loving heart all the days of her life. I'm not saying that my Delaware people don't place a value on a loving heart, but I know Mama thought of it as a Christian virtue. So do I.

The river that flowed through Mama's heart, if I can express it this way, bore the name Amos Reeve. From the time the muscular, graceful, handsome Amos paused along Coon Creek to flirt with the pretty little Whiteturkey girls, Weetdolly, too young to harbor such thoughts, had fallen in love. Oh, how she loved that man. I'm sure that if I'd been paying attention, if I'd known then that I was going to write this book seventy-five years later, I could cite you no end of small tendernesses between those two. But I was a kid and they were my mama and papa. It all seemed unremarkable between them; the way it should be, nothing more. Now it does strike me as remarkable that, for all the differences between Amos and Dolly and the worlds they grew up in, my folks never had a fight in our presence. They'd go off into the woods around our place sometimes to talk things over, especially when the depression started to squeeze the Reeve family pretty hard. But whatever sparks flashed from their frictions came without thunder; Mama allowed all us kids to feel that we were washed over by the sweet melody of an Indian love song.

Mama's work and Mama's love. I accepted them, never questioned them; they supported my world. But Mama's mystery . . . that's another matter. That I've just discovered, thinking about her now, so many years later, as I prepare to put my memories on paper.

I'm not talking about feminine wiles, though Dolly Reeve certainly possessed those. She did all she could to make herself up real pretty when she went to town, even if she had to use the charcoal from a burnt match to darken her brows. I don't think Papa was a sympathetic audience for what he liked to call "women's nonsense." In fact I remember once he found rouge in Mama's bag and threw it out in the field, making a great show of righteous indignation. They were strong, opinionated people, both of them — sometimes strong in their folly. Mama didn't snap back, even under such extreme provocation. What she did was to take her case before the Reeve women and, with the support of Papa's mother and sisters, force Amos into full-scale retreat.

The women on the frontier did what they could to further the feminine mystique, as women have in all times and all places.

But Mama's mystery had to do with the makeup of her personality, not with powders and shadows and such frivolous things. Let me place before you two women—separated by just a few years—and you'll see what I mean. The first is the fourteen-year-old Phoebe Whiteturkey who flirted with Amos Reeve. Raised by Grandma Wahoney, she spoke Delaware fluently. Because Grandma relied on her, she didn't go off to Haskell like her sister Mamie. She had only our local one-room school, and her English was halting and unsure. She worshiped at the Delaware Big House. She wore traditional Delaware camp dresses, bright as flower gardens. She was skilled in basketmaking, weaving watertight baskets from the split bark of the hackberry bush.

The second is the Dolly Reeve I knew growing up. She spoke Delaware with the old people, or when she wanted to keep things from us kids. Her English was better than Papa's—a big vocabulary, very good usage and grammar. She was a loyal Episcopalian, a regular churchgoer, who never attended a Big House ceremony in my lifetime. She wore the latest fashions and favored tasteful black-and-white polka dot outfits. She wove no baskets but was skilled at many crafts, and her bonnets were as neatly made as any basket.

Ten years separate the two women. Ten years and a tremendous act of will. How did my Mama work such a change in herself? She was a highly capable woman, as I think I've made plain. And she must have been fiercely motivated. Therein lies her mystery. What was it that urged her to the transformation, especially when her striking Delaware full-blood looks proclaimed her Indian at the moment of first meeting? I'm not going to be able to answer the question; I don't know if Mama could. But I can make some suggestions.

Surely her marriage to Amos Reeve was one thing that urged her. Not that he would ask her to change or be put off by things Indian. He grew up in Indian country, after all. His brother Hank married Mama's cousin; his sister Shirley married a Cherokee man. And yet things most definitely were expected from the wife of Amos Reeve, from her church membership to her mastery of the domestic arts.

Papa's attitude about Indian things was kind of complicated. He enjoyed the stomp dances and summer socials, actually, as much as Mama. He tried out some of the Delaware ways himself. But he also drew a line for us kids.

I'll give you an instance. The Longbone family lived above our place, on a hill in the woods. We hung out with their kids, visited back and forth, all that. The Longbones were pretty traditional; there were times they held peyote meetings and sweats by their place. The Peyote Church had its followers among the Cherokees and Delawares; I guess you could say it replaced the Big House for a lot of the traditionals. I remember that one time Papa went to one of their ceremonies; he ate peyote with them. I guess anyone who wanted to be part of it was welcome. Anyway, I think it made his stomach sick, mostly. After that, when the Longbones had their church meetings, the Reeve kids were locked safely away inside our house. I had the idea that something dangerous was going on; maybe boozing. There was a good deal of drinking among the Delawares, and we all knew it. But I discovered later that no one ever got intoxicated around the Peyote Church ceremonies. Alcohol was strictly banned from such affairs. And yet we were warned away from the Longbone place only when the traditionals gathered.

Part of the reason for Mama's change must lie in the burial of the Delaware dolls. The dolls were lost on Mama's watch, if I can put it that way. If Grandma Wahoney had handed her dolls on to

Mama, it might have come out different. But she didn't do that; she took the dolls with her into the grave. She was telling Mama that the Delaware time was over, that Mama should live her life in the modern world. "The past is dead; the past is buried. The dolls, which are the health of the tribe, the future of the tribe, are in the ground with me." That was Grandma's last message. I don't know if she was right; as I look back over my life, our lives, I'm not sure she was. But it was a powerful message, and Mama took it to heart. That was another thing.

I probably come closest to understanding Mama's mystery when I remember a look in her eyes. I saw the look when Grandma Reeve brought home my big sister, Indie, and displayed her with a kind of hesitant pride, to show off surprising blond highlights in her hair. It turned out that Aunt Marianne and Grandma Reeve had tried to make Indie look a little more like the cute blond girls who were turning all the boys' heads. They washed her hair and rinsed it in lemon juice. And I guess it did put some touches of blond—more like auburn probably—into her long, dark hair.

I don't remember Mama saying much about it. I do remember her cupping Indie's head in her hands and looking long into my sister's dark eyes. The hurt that was in Mama's eyes, the way she shook her head so slow and resigned . . . it was as if in that moment she opened a window onto a sealed room in her soul. Her look seemed to say that even the best (I know she believed that Papa's people were the best) could be cruel without realizing. I never saw that look again. As far as I know, Mama was comfortable with her life, content with her lot. But sometimes I wonder if she was hiding a hurt and trying to protect us from being touched by the same prejudice.

Mama built some fences. She consented to having Amos keep us in when the Longbones had a peyote meeting. She raised us up in the Episcopal Church. She drilled us in our schoolwork. She sold her wampum belts to buy us school shoes. Maybe she was wrong to do it. Certainly she wasn't able to protect us from insults and scorn. They were in the air, part of our world. Each of us girls married white, like her. And each of us had our own battles with in-laws, like her. Some things are your destiny, no escaping them. But still, you can appreciate a mother's attempt to shield her children.

For the reasons I've mentioned, and some I may never understand, Dolly Reeve backed away from her heritage and taught herself the ways of the white world. She was good at it. But of course you can never transform yourself altogether; it's impossible. Mama remained the girl Grandma Wahoney raised up, and our house was more Delaware than she would ever have admitted.

I think I was closer to Mama than any of the other kids. Here's my reason for saying that: I was in the middle, you see. I was youngest for five years. When the big ones were in school, I was still at home. We had some lovely dinners, just Mama, Papa, and me. I'd sit with them at the table and sip tea . . . just like I was a grown-up. Then the little ones came, and I was the one who helped raise them up. So, yes, I think I was closest to Mama.

Maybe that's why I had more interest in Delaware ways and Delaware talk than any of the others. Mama didn't encourage us to learn Delaware, but she didn't discourage it either. She held Delaware naming ceremonies for the first four. I remember that Ruth's name was Otae, which she told me meant flower. Mine, as I've told you, was Pima Pen Okwe; I've forgotten the others. We didn't do anything official with names for the younger ones, but I stepped in and helped. I'm proud that I managed to learn enough of the old language to give my brother and sisters what I still think are very apt Delaware names.

You see, Mama was always patient to answer my questions. I was curious about the language, enough to be tugging on her sleeve, asking her how to say this or that in Delaware. I'm quite sure I was the only one of the seven children who did it, and I think it gratified her that at least one of us was interested. I guess it meant a lot to me; I judge that from the fact that I've remembered words in the old tongue for seven decades and more.

Let me tell you some stories to finish your introduction to Dolly Reeve. The first offers a glimpse behind Mama's mask. When he was a young teen, my brother Henry became a notorious lazybones. He could spend hours lying about in bed, even in midday, and that drove my father to distraction. Once Papa, who'd been searching and shouting, discovered Henry in his favorite resting place. "Out of that bed now, Henry," Papa shouted. "If you can't be of some use around the house, you can just take your lazy bones out of here." Mama had followed Papa upstairs; I'd gone about halfway up myself, so I heard what she said, not shouting, but unmistakably serious: "If anyone is to leave this house, Amos, it's not going to be Henry." It was Mama's house, after all, bought and paid for from the sale of her allotment land. Besides, Delaware women ran their households. Their husbands came to live with them. And we were still that much Delaware.

The second story features the same cast of characters, expanded to include my big sisters. The house was the site of a typical bustle of activity. Mama had a big kettle of our white wash on the boil and a pot of pinto beans cooking away; Indie and Ruth were helping out with the wash. We heard a high, thin wail coming from beyond our hill; Henry's voice, though I've never heard such pain and terror in it. We dropped what we were doing and rushed out to see Henry running over the hill, holding his hand over his head and screaming.

It turned out that Henry had shot three of his fingers nearly clean off. Henry was about thirteen at the time. He had his own gun, a 13-gauge .410 shotgun, but he really wanted to hunt with Papa's 16-gauge. He'd taken that gun and gone out after rabbits. But it was big and awkward for him; somehow he tripped, the gun hit a stump, fired, and left his three fingers hanging by just a strip of skin. It could have been worse.

Papa heard the screaming; he came riding up on the big gray mare at just about the time Henry arrived. Ruth retrieved her white blouse, soaked it in camphophenique, and wrapped it round the injured hand. Mama fished out her whites and poured the boiling water in the radiator, which was the only way to get the car running in winter. Mama held Henry in her lap, and they raced off to the hospital, where they couldn't do anything but take off the fingers.

Mama must have gotten this idea from Grandma Wahoney; I don't know where else it could have come from. They came back from the hospital with Henry's severed fingers. She straightened them out, tied them to a board, and had Papa bury them out back. We marked the burial and treated it like a grave. The idea was that the missing fingers wouldn't hurt him, the way missing body parts sometimes do, if they were properly looked after.

That wasn't the end of it. I had to lace up Henry's boots, for one thing, for years after, and he made himself just as big a nuisance as he could. The boots were too tight, they were too loose; sometimes I did and redid them three times over. I don't know what pleasure he got out of it, but he was my brother and I loved him, so I put up with it. The more interesting thing that happened after the accident was that Mama had a dream. She dreamed that some critter had dug up the fingers and pretty well devoured them. She took the dream seriously and fretted over it until Papa went to the little grave and exhumed the burial. The board was still there, the straight little finger bones tied neatly in place. Mama was reassured when she saw it. She decided that the vision had been a warning, telling her to take better care of the burial site. From that time on we lavished flowers on Henry's buried fingers. I hope his real grave now is as well tended as that one was.

I'll finish the portrait with what was probably the most traditional moment Mama ever shared with us. Let me tell you about the time Mama ate for Rosie Longbone. What happened was this: Carolyn Longbone, who lived across the creek from us, came by to ask a favor of Mama. Her girl Rosie, dead a year, was hungry and needed someone to eat for her. Would Mama do it? The way Carolyn knew her daughter's spirit was uneasy—hungry was the way she put it—was that odd and near-to-serious accidents had begun to happen to her sons. One had burned himself; the other had cut his foot. Worse things would undoubtedly follow unless the spirit of their dead sister was pacified.

Mama agreed to eat for Rosie—in a sense to become Rosie and accept food on her behalf. The next day Carolyn Longbone came with a big dishpan heaped with her daughter's favorite foods, and Mama did her very best to eat it all. I think it's safe to say now that we kids helped some.

Until I started to think about my Mama as a woman living between two worlds, I'd almost forgotten the episode. I guess when I was a kid it had seemed like one of those things that happens, nothing special. Now, looking back, it captures the essence of the generous, mystical Delaware way, just as it reveals that side of Dolly Whiteturkey Reeve's nature.

Seven

THE REEVES
REVISITED

There are introductions to make. You haven't really met Papa yet, except through Mama's eyes. You've glimpsed Henry on his worst day. Indie and Ruth you know only as my toasty bookends on chilly nights, and Betty as my playmate in dollmaking. Raymond and Amy are as yet unmentioned. My family, which provided sustenance and support, comfort and good company, lessons and play, and which most assuredly made up the greatest part of my small and pleasant universe, awaits you. It's time you got to know the Reeves.

Amos Reeve was a slight, trim, athletic man. Papa was a calf roper, and a pretty good one, at our local rodeos including the famous Dewey Roundup, held each year on the Fourth of July. He truly was a fine figure of a man when he sat Old Brownie — keen, alert, perfectly balanced in the saddle. He wore red, white, and blue pin-striped silks that ballooned out in the breeze as he trotted smartly on parade. We kids would sit in the packed stands with Mama and Grandpa Whiteturkey, who wore the big white Stetson that was his trademark, sipping the big bottles of pop he bought us and swelling with pride as Papa rode by, just as patriotic as Uncle Sam himself.

Papa was a pumper for the oil company by trade. He had a string of pumps and power houses under his care, and he rode the circuit on Old Red, Old Brownie, Old White Eyes, or the Old Gray Mare, who was a giant beast. I don't suppose his horses were really all old; somehow the word worked its way into our names for them. In any case, a succession of "Old So-and-Sos" made their way round his trail of pumps and houses year after year. Papa was a handy man; there was nothing mechanical he couldn't fix, and he kept all that heavy equipment purring. The power house I remember was the one directly on our way to school, where we'd warm up on frigid winter mornings. The house had a big gas engine and a flywheel so heavy that Papa, who wasn't a hefty man, had to jump on it to get it started up. In the middle of that house there was a wheel, must have been fifteen feet around, with mighty rods attached like a big steam locomotive. Those rods drove the grasshopper pumps that bobbed their steel heads up and down pulling pools of oil into the pipeline.

My Papa was fearless. Absolutely. He was a storm chaser, long before there was a name for it. He chased storms for the same reason they do today—the electrifying thrill of it. We have some kind of storms in northeastern Oklahoma. Terrifying storms. Thunderheads turn day into night; lightning rips the black velvet sky with jagged flaming knives; winds flatten the carpet of tall grass and snap limbs as thoughtlessly as children pluck the legs off grasshoppers. Tornado funnels drop from those tremendous storm clouds like teats from the belly of a black sow.

You could smell those storms coming, feel the charge in the air, sense the drop of pressure, watch the excitement build in Papa. Mama, who feared very little, was terrified of lightning. It was something she shared with a lot of Indians. I think it had to do with the fact that, on the plains, any structure stands above the flat and is subject to lightning strikes. In any case, Mama would gather us kids around her and beg Papa to come with us into the dank safety of our tornado cellar. He would pull on his yellow rain slick, saddle up Old Brownie, who was as fearless as he was, and ride out into the driving rain. We'd catch a glimpse of him, an eerie yellow figure in the flashes of lightning, as we scurried along like baby chicks under a tarpaulin held out in Mama's widespread arms. All the time that we sat in the semidark of the cellar, keeping an eye out for scorpions and spiders, Mama would be praying and crying over Papa. I don't think he did it to hurt her. He was a storm chaser is all; it was in his blood to crave that high.

Spring was the prime season for storm chasing. In the fall Papa called what he did duck hunting, but in truth it was much the same. When the chill, needle-sharp rains of November settled on the land, making our tramp to school an ordeal, Papa rode out again in his yellow rain slick to shoot the ducks that flew over in tremendous flocks on their way south. Sometimes he took Henry with him, but most often he went alone, stayed some days, came back with just enough ducks to justify the outing. But I know it was the storm and not the ducks he loved.

Fearlessness stood a man in good stead on the frontier. I remember the day Al Spencer and his gang of ten desperate men robbed a bank in Bartlesville and then scattered into the cliffs and caves in our part of the country. Spencer was a far-famed bad man, a robber of banks and a feared killer. All the Reeves were fishing on Coon Creek when the posse rode up, splashing and scaring away the fish. They were in a fever of excitement; Spencer and his men had led them a merry chase, and they'd caught no one. A few words told Papa all he needed to know about the crisis. He raced home, got his gun, and joined the town men in their search for the outlaws.

We abandoned our fishing and went home with Mama to await the return of our hero. Henry, who still had his ten fingers then, played the role of our protector, sitting bravely in the open with his shotgun cradled in his lap. Mama, who was far the better shot, kept her rifle close at hand. Papa didn't return home until after sunset, hungry, weary, and drained after long hours of a fruitless chase. The posse believed, and father agreed, that members of the Spencer gang still lurked nearby. So he gathered the family into our automobile, and we drove over to Grandpa Reeve's place to spend the night. We didn't want our car seized by outlaws in their escape.

We never did see any of the bank robbers, although a search turned up evidence that one, at least, had been hiding within earshot when the posse rode up to our fishing hole.

Papa in his red, white, and blue rodeo shirt. Papa in his yellow rain slick, dancing to the music of thunder. Papa riding off with the posse to hunt desperate men because it was his duty. Always on horseback, always dashing, always brave. Amos Reeve was a hero to me, in a time and place that didn't produce its heroes, larger than life, on the silver screen but discovered them, wiry and five foot eleven, if that happened to be their stature, in the flesh.

If Papa was our hero, as I believe we would all agree, then it is equally true that his firstborn, Indie, was his little princess. Indie, seven years older than I, was our beauty. Her long dark hair did have lights in it; I can almost sympathize with the impulse of the Reeve women to make her a blond. I don't know if you exactly think of your sister—who was, after all, tangled up in berry bushes, diving and frolicking in our swimming hole, or leading us up and over the pipeline on our high-wire act—as beautiful.

But I do know that Indie was the one I longed to look like. When Ruth teased me pitilessly about my big feet—until I actually stood barefoot with an ax contemplating the pluses and minuses of chopping off my toes—the delicate little feet that so shamed mine belonged to Indie. Of course if her feet were size six, then that's the way feet should be. It's a good thing they weren't size five or I might have swung that ax.

Indie seemed somewhere between mother and sister, always so capable and sure of herself. I remember her taking me to our one-room school when I was starting and she must have been finishing. We'd stop at Papa's pump house and then have to run to make it before the bell stopped ringing. She'd pull me along, and we'd race faster than I could ever go alone. I hardly remember my feet touching the ground on those dashes in pursuit of knowledge.

There is an aptness about these memories of Indie and school. Indie was the one among us who had some college. I believe Papa had plans for her and saw her acting as his polished, cultivated little hostess as the Reeve family emerged from the Coon Creek backwater to play a role in the oil politics of Bartlesville. It could be I'm wrong about that; in any case, fate had a different but not unrelated plan for Indie and our family. My big sister got enough college to teach in one of our local schools; two years and some sort of certificate did the trick. She taught one year, maybe less than a full term. A young fellow from Texas, down Beaumont way, came up to Dewey. The winds of business blew him; he was a car salesman, and there was a lot of new money, oil money, around Bartlesville and Dewey. He was a good-looking boy, smart and ambitious, and he turned a lot of heads. But Delmar Sanders only had eyes for Indie; there was no girl in these parts who could hold a candle to her, truth to tell. In just a few months he coaxed a yes from her, and they got hitched and moved back down to Beaumont. Delmar Sanders had a head on his shoulders and a nose for money. They struggled for a time—he went to law school at night—but soon enough Delmar was a Texas lawyer with political connections I never quite understood. He started buying up property around Beaumont, and in just a few years Delmar and Indie were well propertied and on their way to being rich.

I don't want to get ahead of my story, but I will say that the Texas money tugged on the Reeve family, pulling my second sister and even my Mama down to Beaumont for a time. Of the seven Reeve children, I'm the only one who's lived my life within fifty miles of our home place; the rest scattered. I would say that Delmar and Indie were the force behind our disintegration. Somehow, even when she was my beautiful big sister, carrying the burden of a lion's share of the chores, Indie wasn't really Oklahoma. She looked beyond our home place, beyond our oil towns, even beyond our state borders to find her future. She was destined to lead our family out of rural Oklahoma. I've always loved rural Oklahoma. I was the stubborn one, and I never did care much for Beaumont. But I sure did admire a lot about Indie, and I envied her little feet.

Ruth was the closest of my siblings, young and old, through the eighty-one years we shared on this earth. I admired her skills when I was little, her courage when I was old, her spunk and humor always. Indie and Ruth shared the big bed with me for years, surrounding me with their body heat; but it was Ruth I found myself snuggling up to on those chilly nights.

Ruth was five years older than me; old enough to dazzle me with her accomplishments, young enough to be a playmate. I would badger her to play with me whenever I got the chance. I always felt so very grown up when we played together. Usually we played at dolls. Mama sewed up some lovely little doll dresses from scraps of cloth, and Ruth was very clever at improvising doll bodies from sticks and corncobs and balls of string and such. When dressed up in frilly ginghams with puffed sleeves and full skirts, our dolls did very nicely. Ruth showed me how to paint faces on the wooden dolls, but in a short time I painted better faces than she did. I was always pretty good at taking my time to get the little beauty touches just right. Ruth never seemed to have a lot of time; she was always busy. She rationed out her doll-playing time with me as if it were some precious commodity.

There were reasons for that. The Reeve family needed a lot from Ruth; we relied on her for a range of services—from our summer refreshment to our family history—and she delivered. She was so good at the things she did. She was the one whose sense of adventure and thirst for learning ate up the world of rural Oklahoma and left her hungry for more.

Somehow, Ruth learned how to brew up root beer and bottle it. Now, I'm not saying she introduced root beer to our part of Oklahoma, but it wasn't a familiar taste for the Reeve family until Ruth made it so. This root beer brewing business took place during Prohibition, and rumor had it that moonshine stills were secreted in the abundant caves and hilly hideaways that dotted our countryside. Ruth would pretend to me that her root beer brewery was the closest thing to an illegal still. I think she did it to keep me out from underfoot. There were pots and coiled tubes and the glass bottles she got from who knows where. It all seemed mystifying and a little dangerous to me. I let her mix up her delicious concoction without much interference. She'd stash the dozens of bottles of her sweet brown brew in the cool damp of our cellar, from which they'd emerge on the scorching days of high summer always a delectable fifty-five degrees. I've always enjoyed root beer, and I've drained frosty mugs of A&W to the last drop, but I've never tasted anything quite like Ruth's home brew. It was musty and sweet and altogether wonderful.

One of the great satisfactions of my childhood actually combined two of Ruth's accomplishments. She'd crack open a bottle of root beer for each of us and then pass around her latest batch of photos. Ruth got herself a two-dollar box camera and took all sorts of pictures of the Reeve family at work and play. She was the one among us who seemed to understand that a family's memories would live in albums and boxes of photos or not at all. Ruth was always there, camera in hand, when we mounted up on our horses, went hunting or fishing, picnicked, whatever. And because I loved Ruth so, emulated her, worshiped the ground she walked on, I felt justified in pestering her unmercifully about her camera. From time to time she relented, placed the valuable little box carefully in my hands, repeated her instructions on how to use it in detail, and let me take a shot. Most of our photos of Ruth were taken by yours truly.

A photo I haven't seen in our albums or boxes, but one that's clear in my mind, is a picture of Ruth as mermaid. It was one of the things she did better than the rest of us; Ruth was a champion swimmer. There was a place down toward Dewey where Coon Creek widened and slowed. The town fathers set up a dock and diving board there and kept the water free of snags and rotting logs. We all went swimming there, but Ruth was the acknowledged star. She could do a half-somersault and a back flip from the board, and she looked wonderful doing them. She had a powerful crawl stroke that sliced through the water. I think she tried to make it easy for me, but I never came close to beating her in a race.

One of Ruth's other accomplishments—that affected me very directly—was her mastery of the art of the tease. I'd believe anything she told me, although experience proved time and again just how foolish that could be, and she took full advantage of my gullibility. I've told you about the near tragedy of my too-long toes. Another feature whose length concerned me was my eyelashes. They weren't long enough. Just cut them off, advised

Ruth, and they'll grow back longer. Easier said than done. And, as it turned out, not true. Then there was the question of my freckles. Wash them in stump water, Ruth advised, and they'll fade away. Obligingly, I sought out a hollowed stump with a pool of fetid water and washed away. The water was swarming with mosquito wrigglers; I smeared them on my skin in a thin paste as I washed. Maybe they undid the work of the healing water; in any case, my freckles remained as bold as ever. Time and again, I readily forgave Ruth.

I've never tired of bragging about my big sister, and I'll do it once again, even if she isn't here to glow and blush pink over my boasting. Ruth was a fine rider. She knew where all the berry bushes were and exactly when they came into season. Ruth was Oklahoma, but she was too big for our little corner of the world. She devoured all we had to offer, and it left her hungry for more. When Indie and Delmar showed her the way to an energized, cosmopolitan world down in Texas, Ruth seized her opportunity and followed.

You've met Henry—not at his best, certainly, but as he was. Henry *was* lazy. No doubt about it. He spent more time in the prone position—when the sun was in the sky—than anyone I've known. If you were to judge which direction was the vertical from observing Henry, you might very well be misled.

And yet Henry accomplished quite a lot. Each year, he went for six days to work on road gangs and such, paying off Mama's and Papa's poll tax. Henry was a straight shooter and relentless hunter who was death to a lot more than his fingers. He brought home rabbits and squirrels, quail and partridges, and all in all made an important contribution to our dinner table.

Henry maintained a long, productive trapline as well. He set snares and small jaw traps up and down the creek and in prime spots here and there on the prairie. He became an expert trapper, knowing where the skunks and muskrats and coons and possums lurked and setting just the right traps in the right habitats. You could get good money for pelts in those days, and Henry always had an ample supply of skins stretched on wood frames and hanging on the barn wall to cure. Every so often, he'd tie his precious pelts onto a stout stick, balance it over his shoulder, and walk on down to Dewey, where he had connections with fur traders who paid him well for his treasure. He'd sell the meat in town as well; there seemed to be a market for any sort of varmint. Henry's traplines were chiefly responsible for his reputation as a snappy dresser and quite a hit with the young ladies.

I was just three years younger than Henry, and my brother Raymond didn't come along for another seven years after me, so I was poor Henry's likeliest playmate in a household filled mostly with women. The game I liked best was played with a hoop and stick. Hoop and stick was an old Indian game; only difference was the way we got our hoops. We'd each take the hub from a wagon wheel, maybe ten inches round, and get it rolling by pushing and guiding it with a stick. We both got so good at it that we could keep those hoops rolling on and on, up hill and down dale. There wasn't really any competition to it—Henry was older, bigger, and stronger and, after all, a boy. But I got so I could keep up pretty well, and we'd have some marvelous runs together. Kept us fit, no doubt of that.

Sometimes I got to tag along when Henry tended his traplines. There were practical advantages to knowing just where in our natural playground he'd set his traps—no use catching our feet. And it added excitement to a life that wasn't long on novelty. Once, I remember, it added a little too much excitement. Making the rounds, Henry and I discovered three skunks in separate snares—quite alive and not at all pleased with us. Before we could make a move, the skunks expressed their displeasure in a most distinctive manner. Stinking, irate, and dreading the chastisement we were bound to receive from Mama, Henry and I clubbed those three skunks into the hereafter. They protested as best they could. When we got home, we both reeked. Mama pretended outrage, but I think I saw a smile. I'm not quite sure about that, because she kept her distance, shouting her instructions. We must take off our clothes in the chill of evening. We must place the clothes down by Coon Creek. We must scrub ourselves off in the big wooden tub in the yard. We must soap the clothes and beat them on the rocks, spread them out to dry, and hope for the best. And tonight we could enjoy the privilege, often requested, of eating our supper picnic style, away from the family table.

Henry loved to ride his horse onto the range, and when he couldn't find one of the local boys to come along, he might well invite me. The range was fenced, but it was expected that gates would be opened. Even the cattle were accustomed to finding riders in their midst. Two favorite destinations were Blue Mound, when we fancied the romance of outlaws, and the Osage Hills. Frank Phillips had his fabulous ranch there, and the rolling hills of sage stretched out into forever. When the wind whipped over the hills, we'd give our horses a run, racing the tumbleweed.

Henry kept things stirred up. He was brave, full of fun, a tremendous tease, a staunch defender. When he wasn't recharging his batteries, he was spinning into action like a dervish. I remember Henry bursting onto the scene of my life in the most improbable, electrifying ways.

We girls played house in many settings provided most graciously by nature, and Henry lurked just outside the elegant proprieties of our box socials and formal teas, menacing us as wildness has always menaced civilization in our frontier world.

Two preferred habitations for our games were some old haystacks with cavernous holes eaten out of them by our cattle and great rocky wastes with enormous granite blocks big enough to serve as elegant dining rooms and smaller rocks that could, with great effort, be moved into place as table and chairs. Indie and Ruth and their circle originated the games; I and my circle of school chums eagerly took our place as lesser lights in the ongoing drama.

The rock stages with their mobile props provided the setting for all sorts of dramas. When, in early summer, anticipation of the grand and glorious Dewey Roundup took possession of us, Henry was allowed in our theatricals to enact the part of hamburger vendor. He would gather persimmon leaves to garnish his mud patties, somehow contrive to make a common board look just as much like a vendor's cart as possible, and cry out, "Already ready, already hot, the tastiest burgers is what we got," sounding just as much like a food vendor as he could.

The shadowy stillness of the hay caverns seemed to us a stylish setting suggesting the pomp of high society. The sweet smell of old hay conjured up the heady aroma of scented candles and perfume for us, so we called these hideaways Palm Beach and tried to act accordingly. In "Palm Beach" the ladies of Coon Creek held their teas and coming-out parties. We took the ritual seriously, lost ourselves in it, and were always startled when Henry came bursting in, knocking over the heaps of hay that served as chairs and tables and shouting, "Hogs got your daughter, hoi oi." I never knew where the phrase came from or why he shouted it with such glee. But now, looking back, I think it expressed his resentment at all the girls who dominated his world. Maybe he longed to tell Mama that hogs—half wild and quite fearsome—had indeed "got" one of her daughters, maybe even me. I couldn't really blame him.

I felt somewhat the same way when, after five years of being the baby and enjoying the privileges that went with that position as my birthright, Betty came along to supplant me in all regards. My memories of Betty may be colored by rivalry and jealousy. I remember her as more delicate and beautiful than I was (I think Ruth's photos confirm that, though my girls tell me they don't necessarily agree). I remember her as a frail, sickly child, though some of my specific recollections are quite different. I remember her as Papa's great favorite, though a sober judgment of the facts suggests that my veiled accusation may be unfair to both parties.

Betty was the first sibling who received the honor of a Delaware name chosen by big sister Lynette. I named her Ulepën, Delaware for "onion," though I can't remember the circumstances that made the name seem so right. In any case Mama didn't object, and Ulepën it was. From that time on Mama dispensed with formal naming ceremonies, and the right to hand out Delaware names informally became mine. Little Ulepën and I did become playmates, although our rivalry extended to the fields of play. I've already told you about the game we invented together. If we hadn't been so competitive, neither of us would have taken it anywhere near as far as we did. I'll always be grateful to Betty for the big part she played in dreaming up the game of bears. It called for talents I probably never would have discovered otherwise, and it awakened my lifelong fascination with making things out of clay.

Henry finally got his brother when Raymond came along in my seventh year. I named Raymond KwëshKwëtët, Delaware for "little piggie," though I don't suppose he looked much more like a cute little pig than most babies do. Trouble was, Henry was ten when Raymond was born, and by the time the little fellow became remotely interesting, Henry was near to grown.

For me the youngest two—Raymond and the baby Amy, born six years later when I was thirteen and the oldest girls had already begun to make their own way in the world—weren't exactly playmates. They were something between brother and sister and my children. As the oldest daughter at hand, I was responsible for looking after the little ones. Perhaps the time for play had passed for me, but I wasn't ready for that to happen; I suppose I resented the two who ushered me into the age of responsibility.

When we became adults, we got to know one another. But that isn't the same thing as growing up together in a place and time when we relied on each other almost exclusively for companionship, support, and good times.

Chubby, beautiful baby Amy was my Tipatët—"little chicken"—who was just as lively and nonstop in her movements as a little prairie chicken. By the time Amy arrived on the scene, the winds of change were blowing hard at the four older Reeve children. The rigors of the Great Depression had sent Henry out riding the rails in search of work. Perhaps he never traveled beyond the reach of Mama's concern. He tells me that one time, seated atop a boxcar looking toward the caboose, he heard Mama's voice calling out a warning and turned in time to see the tunnel that might have taken off his head. Maybe so. But certainly he traveled beyond the reach of my companionship, and he never stopped until his wanderings took him to California.

At the same time, the promise of wealth, despite the hardships of the depression, called first Indie and then Ruth down to Beaumont, Texas, where Delmar Sanders was founding his fortune. Even Mama and Papa would follow the well-worn path to the Texas promised land. South of Eden, as I like to think of it, Eden being the rustic Coon Creek settlement where Mama tended her gardens, Papa rode off into the raging fury of Oklahoma storms in his yellow rain slick, Henry set up his traplines, and the Reeve daughters played at being society ladies in houses of straw and stone. For me that innocent place and time has always been an image of Eden. Looking back at my life, I suppose you could say that I've clung to that vision and tried to make it live again in the loving rural communities I've called home.

Eight

WHEN TARZAN CAME
TO COON CREEK

I guess in a lot of ways I've been talking about education through-out this story. No one in my life ever taught me as much as Mama—not anywhere near. Ruth and Henry could claim con-siderable credit, too, if credit is due. All life is a learning, and God has so ordered his world that every bird and bush has a lesson for us. I have been an eager student in that classroom all my life long.

Right now I don't want to talk to you about education, but about schooling, which I think you'll agree is a different matter. We had schooling, of course, probably not too different from what Mama had years before. Our schoolhouse had one room, wooden benches, a slate and chalk for each of us, big tablets, a woodstove, an add-on side room for domestic science, which, after all, was the science we were most in need of knowing. And most important, our school had books. Wonderful books that opened up worlds to us, trapped as we were in our provincial isolation.

School was just a mile away, no more than twenty minutes when we walked slow, stopping at Papa's pump house and idling along, picking flowers on the way. School was no less than twenty minutes when we rode our horses, which was allowed, and stabled them in the shed out back. When we rode, we'd race, tearing up the meadow as we whipped our horses, laughing and shouting.

The horseback riding was frowned on by parents, who considered it a sad and sissified thing to ride a horse a mere mile. So when winter loosed its grip and the road dried past being a river of goop, we'd commence to discover all manner of sprained ankles and pulled thigh muscles—we knew nothing of hamstrings or sports medicine back then, but we knew very well how to fake a limp. I'm sure Mama was on to us, but she feigned concern and grudgingly gave in to our pleas. I'm afraid that sometimes I couldn't contain my excitement and ran to the barn to saddle up Old Brownie.

I was in a hurry to get to school, and not just for the thrill of racing. I really did love school. Or to put it more accurately, I loved to read. Still do, for that matter. I learned to read on the neat little illustrated readers of the time—I believe we had the famous McGuffey, though I couldn't swear to it. I do remember some of the stories I labored over almost by heart. I can sit down today and tell you *The Little Red Hen* word for word the way it was in our reader seventy-five years ago. I worked so hard on those lessons that I took their morals to heart. I suppose the stories we parsed and memorized were a lot like the old Delaware legends in their impact. They taught little lessons of life. Each story had a moral, both in the Delaware tradition and in our McGuffey's Readers.

If you remember, the Red Hen I'm so fond of performed every step of the bread-baking process, from growing the wheat to grinding the flour to mixing the dough, without any help from her friends. But they were ready—more than ready, eager—to help her eat the bread. Under the wise tutelage of the Red Hen, I've noted that same pattern in my acquaintances time and again. And I've enjoyed the hen's ultimate revenge: the chance to enjoy the fruits of my labors in peace and privacy.

The point I'm trying to make, I guess, is that we taught values 70 years ago. And Grandma learned them pretty much the same way 180 years ago. So this thing they call value education isn't anything new. Just a new name. I've found that there are new things, plenty of new things, in the world, but when it comes to people and the way we live, mostly it's new names for the same old thing. If we educated our children and didn't teach them values, now that would be something new. The question, I guess, is Whose values? That's where the controversy comes in. Back in my day, things were simpler; we relied on Bible stories and the Little Red Hen and such, and we came through all right.

One of the great advantages of having eight grades in a single room is that we got to listen to all the lessons. Now that was no particular pleasure for the older kids and may have contributed to their restlessness and boorish behavior. But for the younger kids it was a glorious opportunity. Simply by listening to the big ones recite, we could learn their lessons and—this was the important point—win the right to read their books. It got so I could read two or three grades ahead of my level, which meant that whenever a new batch of books came in, I was one who got to take home the treasures and lose myself in the worlds they opened up. I must have read *Ben Hur* three, four times. The legend of faith pleased me; I'd always gotten my Bible stories straight from the good book. But what really intrigued me was the exotic world of ancient Rome. Could anything possibly be more different from the quiet little backwater I grew up in? Here was pomp and glory and, yes, depravity such as I had never imagined possible. I never could afford to travel much; I've always done my traveling in the world of the mind, between the covers of books.

One year Tarzan swung into Coon Creek, and I was the first to greet him. I don't think I'd heard of Edgar Rice Burroughs or his wild man until the shelf of new books appeared without fanfare on the school library wall. I took one, because that was what I did with new arrivals. And I discovered a kindred spirit. Of course, everything in the Tarzan books was exotic and strange. The jungle plants were like nothing I'd ever seen, and the menagerie of African animals could just as well have stepped off a second ark. I'd heard some of the names before—lion and elephant at least—but had no idea what even those looked like. I was fascinated by the descriptions of the exotic creatures who were Tarzan's familiars. I long suspected that some of the more incredible—the mandrills with their red and purple masks and the twenty-five-foot pythons—were figments of Burrough's imagination, until I met them in zoos.

For all the strangeness, I felt a kinship with Tarzan. He was wild; we were wild. He could have stepped into our wilderness and learned its ways. Easily. I could have climbed up into his canopy of trees and been more at home than that silly Jane ever was. He was raised by animals and spoke with them. Grandma Wahoney knew and spoke with the Otter People when she was a girl, and I firmly believed that was possible. So maybe I read the wonderful Tarzan books—*Tarzan and the Ant Men* and *Tarzan and the Jewels of Opar* and all the rest—with a different attitude than most readers brought to them. I thrilled to the action, as so many other readers did. I also believed in it. I thought Tarzan was real, more real than those monstrous Romans in *Ben Hur.* He showed me that it was possible for a man to live in harmony with the world. He taught me that nature is endlessly fascinating.

It was thrilling to travel to exotic places in books. But my most important journey of the mind didn't take me to the African jungle or anything nearly so foreign. Instead, it took me home—fifteen hundred miles east, back three centuries to the Delaware home place in what had become William Penn's crown colony. The book that took me there was *The Light in the*

Forest. It just made me feel so proud—of who I was, of what my people were like—to read that book. I don't know how many times I read it. When I needed to, I guess, which was pretty often.

The story told of a white boy taken captive and raised by the Delawares. Eventually he was returned to a white settlement. The thing was, he hated everything about colonial life. All he wanted to do was get back to his Delaware family, to live again the life he'd grown up with. The book made our way of life sound so appealing. Really, a lot of the life—the planting, the hunting and fishing, navigating the rivers in dugouts, making most of the things you needed to use, gathering fruits and berries in season, even some of the games and social dances—wasn't so very different from what we ourselves did. I'd heard of the Big House and the Gamwing, but the book told fascinating details I didn't know. It was the first time I realized how religious my Delaware people were, how some of the things we believed weren't so different from the Christian. I won't go on and on; I think you get the idea. I'll just say that when the captive boy did run away from the English and get back to his Indian family, I was right there with him.

A lot of us who went to the Coon Creek school were Delaware; some of our teachers were Indian, too. I don't remember anything much being said about the old Indian ways, except for what was in the textbooks. And those were standard stuff, what everyone was getting. Yet I did learn some things about Delaware history, and it must have come from school. I knew we'd wandered farther than any other tribe, coming from the Atlantic to Oklahoma. We'd kept together for three hundred years, under pressure that broke many other tribes. Our wampum was recognized and valued up and down the coast, by Indians and white settlers alike. I knew we were considered the grandfather tribe, as a mark of respect for all we'd survived. I knew enough to be proud of being Delaware. It's not that I looked down on anyone else—we all pretty well accepted each other. It's just that I wouldn't have traded being Delaware for anything else.

I suppose you could say that the boy in *The Light in the Forest* was one of my teachers in our one-room school. Maybe Tarzan was too, the year he swung into Coon Creek. And come to think of it, neither of them was the strangest teacher I had. Or the best. Or the worst.

Teachers were pretty much catch-as-catch-can in rural Oklahoma. I doubt if there were any degree requirements beyond being one jump ahead of the highest class you taught, which in this case meant some high school. The pay was bad, the problems were monumental, the older students were sometimes surly and disrespectful. Some families supported the teacher and urged respect; the Reeves were like that. But a lot of the parents had no book learning themselves, wanted their kids available for chores, and resented the "civilization" represented by school and teachers. Mama saw book learning as the way for us to claim the promise of America. Papa was an avid reader himself, who used most of the hour he took for lunch to lie in bed reading works of fiction. We were lucky; we went to school excited at the idea of learning. Many of our schoolmates brought their fear and confusion and resentment and came back with just as little as possible.

Let me introduce you to a few of my teachers. I want to give you some idea of the mix of indifference, inability, and—yes—idealism we dealt with. Indifference doesn't come with a name I remember anymore, though there was a time I was prepared to testify against her, by name certainly, before our local magistrate. She was a plain-looking woman of few words and gross habits. I mentioned the little add-on we called the domestic science room. Well, this teacher took that in the most literal sense. She put a cot and a few personal things in the room and took up residence there. She advocated the "turnip" theory of domestic science; she kept a big bag of turnips in her room and fed us liberally from it. In her defense, I must tell you that the turnips were fresh and good. That was as close to teaching domestic science as she ever came, and domestic science was her best subject. Mostly I remember her sitting up at her desk and absentmindedly picking her pimples while we students did whatever we chose. Some of us made ample use of the library and probably learned as much as we would have under better conditions. Others found leisure to be, in truth, the devil's playground.

The situation took a serious turn when some of the older boys, who earned the title delinquent, took one of the girls behind the school, threatened her, and abused her. Our teacher paid no attention, but in time the girl's parents found out. Outrage swept through our rural community and focused on the teacher. The girl's parents wanted her out; my parents and many others seconded the motion. The teacher's response was to make a show of her silver-plated revolver, bring the bag of turnips and whatever other food she could muster into the domestic science room, and barricade herself inside. She issued her own ultimatum: she would not relinquish her post until she received full pay for the entire school year. The parents were not ready to give in to such nonsense; neither were they willing to face her pistol in an effort to resolve the issue. So they took the refuge of the law-abiding and brought the case before the local judiciary.

I was one of the students scheduled to take the stand and describe a steady educational diet of turnips and acne, spiced by indiscretions ranging from card playing to sexual liberties perpetrated by the sons and daughters of the soil. I was all dressed up in my Sunday best, and I rehearsed in my mind just what I was going to say. I wish I could tell you I did my civic duty with courage and eloquence, but I never had to get up on that stand.

Some compromise was reached, and the siege of the domestic science room was lifted. Our diet tended more to learning and less to turnips for the rest of that year.

Inability still has a name—Miss Golden—and a lovely face in my memory. She was a cute little redhead then, more than cute, a blooming frontier beauty. She couldn't have been over twenty years old, probably more like eighteen. She was put in charge of a roomful of children ranging from six to very near her own age. Some of the eighth-grade boys were fifteen, even sixteen, big strapping fellows. Who gave little Miss Golden the keys to this unenviable kingdom? Parents who couldn't find anyone else willing to take on the job for so little pay, I suppose. Parents who must have thought that anything was better than nothing. Parents who certainly didn't come and offer any day-to-day assistance while the inevitable drama unfolded.

Teachers had few weapons in their arsenals in those days. They were alone in cramped, hostile places, with children who would far rather be out at play in wide open spaces. They had readers and slates and dry histories to offer against the lure of sun and soft spring breezes. They had rulers and rods and license to use them, but was slim little Miss Golden likely to take the rod to the backsides of big, work-toughened country boys? They had the boiled potatoes and pots of savory pinto beans that most teachers provided as supplement to the bag lunches we brought from home. Miss Golden cooked up potatoes and beans with the best of them. She offered the big girls beauty hints, ways to touch up hair, to add glamour to eyes. She was popular with the big girls. But she offered the big boys a target for the leering and boasting that are such a part of growing up to be manly men.

All year she fought an uneven battle with the big boys for control of the school. Maybe the way she dressed was part of the problem. Miss Golden dressed like a young lady; she wore skirts, and her bloomers peeked out from beneath. On the day that turned out to be the last day of school, the big boys took off Miss Golden's green bloomers and ran them up the school flagpole. I felt so terrible for her that day. I felt bad for us, too. If she was unable to control a school, we were incapable of controlling our worst natures.

I don't want to end on such a note. The worst doesn't represent who we are. The best comes closer. I believe we dwell too much on our worst, when we really have much more to learn from our best. For our little school, the best certainly were Rabbit Williams and his wife May. They'd come to us from Dewey, where Rabbit was a high-school coach; in our little school they divided eight grades between them. May brought along a police dog and a furry little Chihuahua. They were an odd couple, but somehow well suited—the dogs I mean; there was nothing odd about Rabbit and May. The dogs were adopted by all the schoolchildren. The couple came to be very special to me, my favorite people in the world besides my own family.

I owe that, I suppose, to Ruby Wittenburg, my best friend in the wide world and my dining partner at school. Every day we ate together. Not only boiled potatoes and pinto beans—they were by no means our only sustenance in the long 9 A.M. to 4 P.M. school day—but also sandwiches and cakes and all sorts of things from home. Partners would swap delectables from the bags their mamas packed. I always thought that Ruby's mom was the best cook in the whole county, after my own. So we ate very well, Ruby and I. I remember one of the sandwiches we created without, so far as I knew, any influence from the outside. We took biscuits and filled them with crisp bacon and slices of tomato. No one else in our part of the world ate them. So if you can't trace the bacon and tomato sandwich to an earlier date than 1925, you can attribute its creation to Lynette and Ruby.

Ruby Wittenburg was May Williams's cousin, which worked out very well for me. When they had Ruby to visit, they'd invite me too. Often they let us spend the night; Papa made an exception to his rule when it came to Rabbit and May. They treated us so very special. When there was a carnival anywhere nearby, we'd hop in their car and drive over. Rabbit Williams was just a champion at carnivals. Whatever the game—shooting, ball toss, breaking balloons, sinking baskets—he could do it better than anyone. We'd come home with all the prizes we could hold in our arms. And when there weren't any special entertainments, we'd gather round May in her kitchen and she'd show us how to make fudge or popcorn. What feasts we'd have!

Rabbit and May were wonderful in school, too. Rabbit actually got me to learn my multiplication tables, and that was no easy task. He even got me to understand fractions. I have a confession to make. As good as I was at reading, I was just that bad at math. It was like there was a hole in my brain where math ability should have been. Papa would try to help me learn, but my ignorance outlasted his patience, and I'd emerge from our sessions in tears, just as confused as ever. But you couldn't wear out Rabbit Williams's patience. He'd work with me and work with me, and finally the light started to dawn. I'm not saying I ever got to be very good at my old bugaboo, but I certainly can balance my checkbook, and I'm not cheated in stores. I get along in the world, mathematically speaking, and I owe that to Rabbit Williams.

When school was calm, well ordered, and under control, it could be very pleasant. We children had a great capacity for play. We knew many ways to make the time pass happily. There were horse races in spring and fall. And we played jacks and jump rope. All our girls seemed to have wonderfully nimble hands and feet. I mean, we were up to foursies and fivesies in jacks. And most of us could jump double Dutch and do all sorts of tricks. I just wish I could remember some of the jump rope rhymes. Sometimes when my granddaughters are fooling around, I catch a snatch of rhyme that sounds a note in my memory. Are they jumping to the same rhymes I did? That seems remarkable to me, but I don't remember well enough to be sure. In winter, when there was snow cover, which isn't too often in Oklahoma, we'd haul out our sleds and boards and snowshoes and such and have a high old time. There was one young fellow who was kind of stuck on me. In winter he'd bring his sled out and drag me around the schoolyard. I certainly enjoyed the attention.

There's a game I'd like to mention; maybe you've played something similar. We called it "ante over." What you'd do is gather on one side of the schoolhouse, throw the ball over the roof, and run off chasing it. Whoever got the ball ran around frantically tagging the rest of us with it. It was a great excuse to race about until you just collapsed on the ground gasping.

I'll leave the little scholars of Coon Creek on the playing field, under the watchful eyes of May and Rabbit Williams. An oddly matched pair of hounds race along with us, yapping at our heels. We were healthy, exuberant, self-reliant; some of us eager to learn. We were also isolated and ignorant. When wise, kind, idealistic people like Rabbit and May Williams watched over us and protected us from ourselves, life could be very good.

Good schooling comes from good teaching. That's always been true, and never more so than in our little one-room schoolhouses. And I think that even in rural Oklahoma, good schooling is an important part of a good education.

Nine

A DAY MUCH LIKE
THE OTHERS

"Lynette." The familiar voice filters through layers of sleep, like light shimmering through deep water. I answer by pulling the covers up over my head. For a few moments, blessed silence. Then, again, "Lynette." This time the voice has grown an elbow. I'm not awake enough to know whether it's Betty next to me or Ruth from across the bed. Ruth's is heavier, Betty's sharper. Either will do the trick. I stumble out of bed. Sun's up; Mama's working near the foot of the stairs, calling my name from time to time as she gathers the fixings for a big pancake breakfast. It's six o'clock maybe, a few minutes after sunrise, a few more minutes after Mama rises. I don't think I've ever been up before Mama; she's our rooster.

"Wash up, honey," Mama suggests. "Pretty soon all the sleepy-heads'll be rising." One of the good things about getting up early to help with breakfast is that you get to spend a little time at the washbasin. Papa or Henry hauled in water from our well last night, and a bucket is standing next to the basin, right by our big woodstove. Because it's near the stove, you don't have to break ice off the surface, but it's still chilly. When I get to it, at least it's clean. We've been taught to conserve water; to this day I kind of shudder when I see a tap just running. I mean, when you've had to carry it up from a well that didn't seem any too close—and in the winter haul big water barrels in a horse-drawn sledge from a deeper and more distant well—you hold on to the understanding that water is a precious commodity. Using just as little as possible, I'd wash up and then slip into my clothes, huddling close to the stove for warmth. By this time Mama has all the breakfast fixings on the table, and the rest of the family is stirring.

I'm considered the best pancake maker among all the kids, and I'm kinda proud of that. I've always been good on the griddle: quick, well organized, accurate. I probably developed my skills whipping up flapjack breakfasts for all the Reeves. We'd use the gas stove because you wanted the black cast-iron skillets to heat fast and even. When we had a pitcher of buttermilk we'd use that with the flour and eggs and baking soda. I knew the quantities without measuring. Mama'd get all the griddles hot, and I'd whip up a big batch of batter. She'd spoon, I'd flip—we were a regular production line. There were times when we made a dozen pancakes for Papa and the same for Henry. The girls, of course, ate a little more modestly, though I'd swear Ruth sometimes came pretty close to that amount. The plates would empty just as fast as we could fill them, until finally the bowls emptied just as the bellies filled. Then Papa would head out to his pumping station after sweeping us all into his arms for a hug. Ruth and I washed dishes while Mama packed up all our lunches, and by 8:30 we were off to school ourselves.

It's late November—brisk in the morning but clear of snow. Many of our school mornings are like this: the sky slate gray, the ground nearly frozen, steam billowing from our mouths as we hurry along toward school. We have to hurry because we want to stop for a warm-up at Papa's pumping station. We know he's had time to hurry on ahead and get his big gas furnace turned on. We're pretty well bundled against the cold, and the furnace is more or less an excuse for one more chance to see Papa before the long school day commences. We make a great show of shivering when we troop in to see him, and he plays along, encouraging us to warm our hands at the furnace. Finally he hurries us out, just in time to line up in the schoolyard for our grand entry.

Today one of the mothers who plays piano has walked her children to school and stayed to play us an entry march. It's a special treat when a mother serenades us this way on the school piano; otherwise we clomp in to a Sousa march or some other band music on the phonograph. We line up pretty much by height. The little ones turn to the rows of small desks up front; those in the middle grades like me take our place at larger desks in the middle of the room; the seventh and eighth graders sit in the big desks at the back of the long room. To complete the geography of the classroom, there's a big slate board at the very front. A series of large maps pull down from slots just above the blackboard. We have the world, the U.S.A., and the state of Oklahoma as they were understood to be in 1920. The teacher's desk comes next, then two long benches where we're called to recite, class by class. The convenient thing about benches is that just about any size bottoms fit them comfortably. On the wall over the blackboard is the very latest flag, with forty-eight stars.

We rise to recite the Pledge of Allegiance: "I pledge allegiance to the Flag of the United States of America and to the Republic for which it stands; one nation indivisible, with liberty and justice for all." That was the official language then, though I promise you that my part of the country couldn't have been more delighted when "under God" was added quite a few years later.

We had subjects, even in our one little room. In addition to the three R's there were civics and history and spelling and, yes, science too. And eight classes had their chance to recite every day. So the nine to four o'clock school day really didn't allow us all that much time. There was an hour given to lunchtime for eating and play, and we had recess in the morning and afternoon unless the weather was just terrible. So the teachers had to hurry us through our paces each day, giving each grade a half hour to forty-five minutes of recitation time.

The rest of the day we could prepare our lessons, which really didn't require all that much effort, or we could listen to all the recitations and learn as much as possible from all the grades. The best of us were soon reading and retaining the work of several grades beyond our own. Of course, by the time you reached the upper grades things had become very repetitious. Maybe that's why teachers had so much trouble with the big boys, though, since many of them were operating three and four grades behind their true levels, that doesn't seem very likely. One of the consequences of this arrangement is that those of us who paid attention really learned our lessons. I mean, we never forgot what we studied in school, even if some of it was more than a little foolish.

I'm in the sixth grade, and we're not scheduled to recite until the afternoon. Our teacher changes the grade order every week so we don't get in too deep a rut. The seventh grade leads off this week, and they're working on a civics unit about the history and government of Oklahoma. This is stuff I'm going to need to know in order to graduate, so I pay close attention. Every student has to pass a test on the state constitution and how statehood brought the virtues of democracy to what had been a wild place, the last refuge of the tribes. I believed firmly, then, that statehood had been a kind of salvation for all Oklahomans. I was surprised to learn, years later, that the Cherokee Nation was very much a tribal democracy with its own legislature and courts, and more civilized than neighboring Kansas and Texas. It never occurred to me when I was a child that the white folks might have reasons of their own for telling us Indians the history they wanted us to learn. Teachers, I was certain, were tellers of truth.

Grandma Wahoney (Ma Wah Taise)

Grandma Wahoney seated between Mamie Whiteturkey Thaxton (*left*) and Phoebe (Dolly) Whiteturkey Reeve (*right*). Held by Grandma Wahoney are Gladys Thaxton (*left*) and Indie Adeline Reeve (*right*).

Phoebe (Dolly) Whiteturkey Reeve, age twenty-five, with daughter Lynette.

Amos Reeve, at about age twenty, riding Old Cadwallader at Coon Creek.

Lynette Reeve, age four, wearing one of Dolly Reeve's hand-sewn dresses.

The Reeve family (*left to right*): Amy, Amos, Lynette, Dolly, Ruth, Henry, Raymond.

Lynette and Gordon Perry, shortly after marriage.

Lynette and Gordon Perry, 1943, in Lincoln, Nebraska.

Lynette Perry, 1943, sitting under the Caney River Bridge in Bartlesville, Oklahoma.

Dolly Reeve, walking purposefully
in Beaumont, Texas

Amos Reeve, in his late forties,
living in Texas.

Grandmother Dolly Reeve with Jackie (*left*) and Linda (*right*), 1957.

Jackie (*left*) and Linda (*right*) with Buster the Wonder Dog, 1957.

Lynette and Gordon Perry at home in the early 1960s.

Left to right: Lynette, Ruth,
and Amy, 1968.

Lynette in London, 1977,
standing in front of Big Ben.

Lynette and Gordon Perry at home, 1978.

Next up are the first graders, who are so cute and funny with their attempts to read that you have to listen to them. I've been working with little Sarah Coonfield, who just can't seem to get the hang of reading. I think she's made a little progress, and I'm hoping her recitation won't be the agony of stammering and guessing it usually is. I feel myself getting nervous as her turn approaches, which is kind of ridiculous because I don't think she cares all that much about it herself. Now the teacher nods toward Sarah. She fidgets a little and then starts out. "The tor . . . the tor, tor. . . ." She's stuck right away. Sometimes these first-grade readers aren't all that easy. "Tortoise, darling," the teacher prompts. "The tortoise says to the hare, 'How would you like to have a race?' " Well, good for her. That's the best Sarah's done in her little life. I'm proud for her.

Now I have no interest in the recitations until recess. So I slip soundlessly to the library shelf and pick up one of my old favorites, *Tarzan of the Apes*. I know the story almost by heart, and pretty soon I'm lost in the jungle, where I remain until the recess bell.

Recess is a whirl of jump ropes. It's the start of a sort of contest that we'll carry through until end of term, now and then, weather permitting. Today weather permits. There's nothing formal about it, yet by May we'll all agree about who's best and next and down the line. Today we're showing off our number one routines on a short rope. Ropes are spinning all over the yard. We're chanting rope rhymes, really only a few, but so out of sequence that it sounds like bedlam. The boys have brought out all the softballs and inflatable balls they can find. They seem to be having some kind of kickball game, but a whole lot of their balls are heading in our direction. Now it really sounds like bedlam. We're screaming a lot louder than we need to, because we want to bring the teacher out into the schoolyard to establish order. She's a woman, kinda young, still new to us, and the sound of girls' voices raised in anguish ought to rally her to our defense. But no, she stays put indoors. Apparently she doesn't want to make enemies of the big boys before it becomes absolutely necessary. Weak. That's too bad. It's going to be tough to get in all the jumping we want, now that the boys have a free hand. But it doesn't surprise us; it's been this way before.

I can hardly wait for lunch. Ruby told me she and her mama were gonna whip up some new dessert, something with popcorn and marshmallows and molasses, and if it worked out, she'd bring it along to share. At recess she'd just given me a tease, rolled her eyes and rubbed her tummy and said "mmm, mmm" just as tantalizing as she could manage. It turned out that her act didn't do the real thing justice. We ate our lunch together as usual, then Ruby motioned me to follow her out into the woods. "Thish sho good, I can't let everyone know 'bout it," she spluttered, her mouth sounding full up. We went all the way to Coon Creek before she thought it was safe; I had to keep a close eye on her to make sure some of that popcorn dessert made its way into my mouth.

Boy, when we finally got to eat it, that popcorn treat really was good. Turned out they used maple syrup on the balls and dipped them in maple sugar. They were so sweet, it was a good thing I didn't have a cavity in my teeth or it would have about blown the roof of my mouth off. We dipped our hands in the creek and drank it down. To this day I don't remember eating anything that tasted quite so wonderful. I think Ruby and I cemented our friendship sharing those maple popcorn balls.

The sixth grade is scheduled to recite second this afternoon. I'm not worried about reciting; I enjoy it, really, except for blackboard work on long division. That can be embarrassing. And since some of the big kids consider me a show-off for mastering their reading lessons, they give me a hard time when I flub the math. Fortunately, today we're reading from the history book, and I don't think I'll have any trouble with that. As it turns out, I don't. We're reading about the Middle Ages, which can be a favorite subject when it comes in the King Arthur legends but certainly isn't in this dry history. I get through it pretty well, fumbling a couple of names but doing it quickly enough so the teacher doesn't correct. I don't think she knows how to pronounce them either.

We're able to get our rope jumping in during the afternoon recess. The boys really don't care much about it one way or the other; what they did this morning was just to show that they could. I've practiced my routine, but for some reason I stumble once anyway. Oh well, you can't be good at everything.

The last hour, after recess, is the longest of the day, especially if you've already recited. As teacher hurries to put the last grades through their paces, waves of unrest begin to roll up from the big boys' section and to wriggle back from the little tykes up front. They tend to meet about where I'm sitting. Big boys reach out and tug your hair, bluster and flirt any way they can. Sometimes you get home to find they've left a deposit of gum or something worse behind. The first- and second-grade boys find a way to turn around and throw spitballs or fire pebbles out of pea shooters. The weary teacher keeps her eyes on the prim little fourth grader who's stumbling through her lesson and shuts her ears to the tumult. The thought occurs to me yet again—the world would really be a wonderful place if it weren't for boys. Finally, the big hand of our wall clock makes its way to twelve, the little hand rests securely on four, and we're out the door.

I usually rush home, racing Ruth and Betty. It's hunger that drives us; after our vigorous play at noon and recess, even the big lunches Mama packs have left us on empty. Today, having stuffed myself on Ruby Wittenburg's popcorn balls, I'm not starving as usual. Still, my sisters are off to the races, and I'm not about to be left behind. Ruth is holding Betty's hand and hauling her along, so with a last-minute burst of speed I get to the door first. I'm hit with the fragrant aroma of fresh baked bread, still warm from the oven. Mama knows we come home from school hungry and have heavy chores to do before supper, so she always has some sort of treat ready for us. She bakes wonderful whole wheat bread. There's a freshly sliced loaf on the table, tall glasses of milk topped by a skin of sweet cream, newly churned butter, and a jar of plum preserves. I've discovered my appetite somewhere along the road home, and I down the bread and jam with gusto. Betty and Ruth have big white mustaches; I can't help laughing at them. Ruth produces our hand mirror, and of course my mustache is the biggest of all.

Before we can sit down to supper, we girls have to gather the eggs. Now, Mama has many hens, and they have the run of the place. They don't lay only in the henhouse; we're just as likely to find eggs in the barn, even under the house. I'm not crazy about searching under the house for eggs. It's not that the crawl space is low; you can almost stand up under there. But varmints sometimes hole up under our house. I've come face to face with possums, skunks, even snakes. All those critters have a fondness for hen's eggs, and I don't relish wrestling ours away from them. Some of the snakes in these parts are poisonous. I've never seen any under the house, but you never know. So I'd just as soon turn over that part of the search to one of my sisters. But Ruth is too much the lady and Betty's too much the baby. Falling in between those unfortunate conditions, I'm the one to play the part.

One thing you have to understand is that hens don't lay for our benefit. They have other plans for their eggs, other destinations in mind beside our skillets. So they often take exception to our impudence in helping ourselves to their posterity. I've been pecked badly about the hands by irate hens. I've learned that one thing you never want to do is put your face or eyes within striking range of their bills. There is a skill to egg gathering; I cover the hen's eyes and head with my left hand and scoop out the eggs with my right.

We make a contest out of the gathering. Each of us takes a big split ash basket, an old Delaware basket, and we see who can gather the most eggs. Since Ruth searches the henhouse, Betty does the barn, and I'm stuck with under the house, my third place finish is pretty much preordained. But it turns out that the hens haven't been scared off by snakes or possums and have found the shadowy stillness under the house appealing; I have a pretty full basket by the time I emerge into the light. After a count, we find that I'm close, but still third.

Henry has returned home to his principal chore—milking the cows. I'm not a very good milker and only do it when Henry's off somewhere. Henry is quick and sure-handed and finishes just about the same time we get the eggs counted and packed away. We store big wooden buckets down in the well, where the cold water keeps the milk fresh. I help Henry carry the pails full of fresh, warm milk to the well. As he hauls up the heavy wooden buckets, I carefully skim the cream from our new supply. Tonight we're going to churn a fresh batch of butter.

By the time we're done, food is on the table. Henry and Ruth have chased down some jackrabbits, and Mama's prepared a rabbit stew. She's added some of the root crops that we store in the barn—potatoes, carrots, wild onions—and the result is simply delicious. We bow our heads and Papa says grace, then we dive into the tempting meal. I mop up every bit of that rich gravy with thick chunks of the whole wheat bread. I'm washed over by a wave of contentment; I say a special little prayer of thanks for my good life.

In the evening I love to curl up with a book. It's not all that easy to read in our gaslit home. There's a wavery, shadowy quality to the light, and you have to get pretty close to a lantern to see the print. Papa loves to read and keeps a big bookshelf filled with O'Henry and Zane Grey and—for me—Gene Stratton Porter. Porter wrote romances for young girls: lots of young love, but lots of action and adventure too. I'm in the mood for one of those exciting romances, because I'm not planning to sit and read. Instead, I'm going to read as I work.

We don't have a churn, but Mama has come up with an ingenious way to make butter. She pours the fresh cream into a heavy earthenware jar, seals it up tight, and sets it on the treadle of her Singer sewing machine. Then, as she sews, working the treadle with her foot, she also churns the butter. Tonight there's no sewing to be done, but we are in need of a new supply of butter. So I've volunteered to work the treadle as I read. I've come to a very exciting part of the book. The young heroine turned detective sneaks into an abandoned and very dusty haunted mansion trying to solve a crime that has her father in prison. Every step she takes is fraught with peril. I work the treadle without even thinking about it as I creep along on the dangerous mission. By the time we've solved the case, I've also made our butter.

A full day. A satisfying day. Great food, hectic play, satisfying work. It all seemed so natural; I had no idea then how terribly hard it would prove to be to strike such a perfect balance in life. Looking back, I think we realized some sort of ideal in our Coon Creek childhood that I've never attained again. Then, it was simply the way we lived.

Ten

READING THROUGH
THE CALENDAR

They follow one after the other, days like the one we just shared. In all sorts of weathers, of course. Some with embarrassments instead of triumphs, tears replacing laughter. But most are like ours—purposeful and playful, in harmony with the demands and pleasures of the world around.

I suppose our country lives weren't all that different from the way my Delaware forebears lived for hundreds of years: in touch with nature, alive to ancient rhythms as migrating birds are. The cycle of the seasons shapes our lives, as it did theirs. As the earth sweeps round the sun, the paths we walk and ride every day—to school, to the creek, to our forts and playhouses north and south, to the woods and the prairie, to town—are transformed again and again to green, to brown, to bare.

We'll walk those familiar paths and pause to see and smell and taste the changes time makes. However far we crawl or fly about the surface of our planet, the greatest trip any of us ever takes is the one we all take together, riding the earth as it whirls on its orbit around the sun. That is the journey we'll be on as we explore the ways the passage of days transforms the tiny corner of the planet I know best.

It has become possible, as it was not when I grew up, to close the window on this most glorious of all journeys. We can follow the sun by plane now, living north in summer, south in winter. We can pull down a glass and concrete blind, heated in winter and air conditioned in summer, streets swept of leaves in autumn, plowed of snow and salted in winter. That is the world most of us want, the world we've labored so hard to create.

How grateful I am that the world of my childhood was too "primitive" for that. We embraced the wonder of the seasons as God created them, surrendered ourselves to their rhythms. We pressed our faces to the glass, kept our senses open, and didn't miss a trick.

When you travel a circle, you can start anywhere. We'll begin with spring, with the season of birth, remembering that the choice is arbitrary, that we could just as well start with winter. Somehow I find that thought consoling.

Spring. The season when the warm sun kissed frozen roads and turned them into muck that couldn't be driven and could barely be walked. A season of storms. Some for show: a dance of lights at evening, jagged rips in the sky, thunder applauding, Mama and children racing to the storm cellar by that light while Papa finds his yellow rain slick and rides out. Some for real: announced by green rolling clouds and machine-gun bursts of hail, limbs snapped from trees. the screams of terrified horses, Papa leading wife and kids to the storm cellar. The fury of those storms was heard, not seen, muffled by dirt walls and amplified by corrugated tin. Papa always took along an ax and crowbar when he went down into the cellar with us. He wanted to be able to pry up the trap and chop his way out in case a tree—or our house—came crashing down. Papa didn't cotton much to being buried alive, as he'd tell us while the storm raged, a smile creasing his lips. It never happened. We were always able to raise the door, to climb out again into the storm-cleansed air, to assess whatever damage wind and storm-tossed tree limbs had wrought. But good fortune didn't argue Papa out of his precautions; he brought the crowbar and ax every time.

In spring, Coon Creek became a torrent of snowmelt and rain runoff. It rose over its banks and spread out on the bottomland. The flood was a blessing; not a Nile flood, but still a renewal of the land that brought forth a bumper crop. And yet the water carried a threat; if it rose too high or too fast, it could surge into the house, even force us out. We kept an eye on the creek all spring, and sometimes at high water we'd post one of the kids on watch. Mama had bedrolls and clothes and food packed up, ready to carry out, and we had a standing arrangement with Grammie and Dad—Grandma and Grandpa Reeve—to wait out the flood in their big house in Dewey if need be.

So God rang in spring with thunder and flood—with his biggest, most dramatic effects—and followed them with flowers. Our dry, brown land bloomed violet and red and yellow and pink, and above all green as the bluestem and turkey foot and Indian grass burst through the ground on their way to towering over my head. I think now that the purpose of the storms and floods was the flowers, which I suppose is another way of saying "April showers bring May flowers." There's a little more to it, though. The thing that intrigues me is the idea that very large causes can have small, exquisite effects. A shy clump of violets, peeking out from a moss bank, follows a storm that shattered tree limbs. The small redeems the large, peace follows violence. That's the pattern I learned in childhood, every time spring dressed the countryside in flowers.

Mama loved flowers. She'd send us out to gather the delicate blooms of spring—violets, wild roses, Dutchman's breeches, cactus flowers—and we'd bring back armloads for the blue delft vases that were Mama's pride. One thing we tried hard not to do was pick any of the little white strawberry blossoms that carpeted damp, low nooks and dells. Before we went out on our own, Mama would take us — she would do this every year — out into the woods to point out the strawberry patches. "These little flowers will be luscious berries in a month," she would say. "That's the time to pick 'em."

The arrival of flowers in the house announced the season of spring cleaning. There might be a new coat of paint indoors or of whitewash out. There would be a thorough washing of walls, a dusting of cupboards, an airing of linens. We would scour the storm cellar and patch up cracks in the concrete. We'd tighten up the shutters and the doors, slap mortar on the cracks in roof and walls that had opened up under winter's pounding. We packed away the heaviest winter clothes in mothballs. I could go on, but I guess our list wasn't too different from most folks' preparations for spring.

Of course I pitched in, we all pitched in, doing whatever tasks were assigned; there wasn't any arguing about that. In fact, I did my chores quickly and well, with what might have passed for enthusiasm but was really something quite different. I wanted to get on to the spring cleaning that meant much more to me.

As you know, we kids had playhouses of all sorts scattered about the neighborhood. Some of them were massive things made out of rock, some elaborate miniatures made out of mud, but all of them were hit hard by winter and required repairs. As the hours of daylight lengthened and the X's on our calendar approached the last Friday in May, the task of fixing up our play houses became pressing.

Below our place, on the Longbone property, the Coon Creek kids had put up a stone fort. I mean, this was a solid fort; some of the outposts that guarded the Old West likely weren't made any better. But every winter, ice would get between the cracks and knock down a portion of one of the walls. I was big enough to make repairs, though it did mean hefting some sizable rocks over my head. We used mud for mortar; the muck there dried hard and held up through the hot, dry summer. We even spread mud over the rocks to create an adobe effect. I wasn't big enough to make the refinements I wanted inside. We'd hauled boulders and tree stumps to set up seats and firing posts in the fort.

The fort was the scene of furious games of cowboys and Indians. The "cowboys" defended the fort, the "Indians" attacked. We'd take turns being one or the other; it didn't matter if you were Delaware or white, only whether you felt like running or sitting. It's true that the "cowboys" got to play local heroes—Tom Mix, Will Rogers, and Tim McCoy were favorites—while the "Indian" attackers were anonymous. Of course it's also true that in Oklahoma some of the famous cowboys really were Indians, but that's a refinement we didn't consider.

What we'd do to ward off attackers was stockpile old, dry corncobs and hurl them at the hostile "Indians"; you didn't just rush our fort without having a pretty good plan. The usual strategy was to lay siege to it. We'd stockpile sweet yellow plums to feast on when we were waiting out a siege. So what you wanted was as much comfort as possible. I'd sketch layouts for where to put the interior furnishings, but I wasn't strong enough to move things into place. I had to ask the Longbone boys for help with that. They didn't mind.

Up above our place, among the cliffs and caves, we set up some pretty hefty rock tables, chairs, and divans on massive flat rock platforms. This was the stage where we girls enacted our dramas—from society teas to circuses and carnivals. Usually you didn't have to do much rearranging here; even the strongest winds didn't push these props around. It was just a matter of cleaning up debris—sometimes you'd find some pretty big branches cluttering our ballrooms and circus tents. If I had time,

I'd scour the moss and lichens and spiderwebs from the rocks. This was our stage, and I didn't like it messy. And because we did enjoy our comfort, we made a point of covering the "chairs" and "couches" with a soft bed of moss.

Our Palm Springs required a lot of attention. Winter didn't do our old haystacks any favors. Many had fallen; all were soggy, mildewed, and smelly. We did a kind of inspection, and we didn't do it alone. We'd poke a long stick into the eaten-out hollows, stir things up, and if the walls didn't crumble, one of us tentatively put a head in. These hay caves had collapsed on us, a messy, scary ordeal at best. Ruth pulled me out by my feet once, and I was grateful for it. We wouldn't be able to do much in these intimate little rooms until the summer sun dried them and the crawly things grew wings and flew away. For now it was an anticipation of things to come.

The houses and furnishings and "bear" families Betty and I modeled from the Coon Creek clay usually didn't survive the spring floods and had to be remade. We had a new creation each spring. I suppose that was a good thing; Betty and I each grew older and better year by year. It got so we'd take pages from the big Montgomery Ward catalog down to the creek and model our household furnishings after what we saw. Our bears got to be so good that our friends started to recognize themselves a little in the dolls we made. As I think back on it, the work with clay was my favorite part of spring.

As Mama promised, the delicate little white flowers soon became sweet, juicy strawberries. We'd been watching their progress, and we arrived at the berry patches, baskets in hand, before birds and bunnies could get too many. Strawberries were the first of an abundant harvest of wild fruit that gladdened our meals for a long season and—transformed by Mama into a luscious array of jams and preserves—sweetened the meals of winter as well.

Let's jump ahead and review the calendar of nature's bounty: The strawberries of May hugged the ground. In June the riches moved into the trees; mulberries so thick with deep purple fruit that we loaded buckets and still the trees were full. The berries stained our bare feet; Mama set out a bucket at the door for us to wash in while mulberries carpeted the ground. Small yellow wild plums, syrupy and sweet, grew in thickets on the prairie in June and July. We stockpiled those plums in our fort and gorged ourselves, not noticing that we'd played through dinner. The sticky syrup on our hands and arms drew flies. The blackberries of August were thickest in Grandpa Whiteturkey's garden. Picking them provided a great excuse for a visit. In September the woods bloomed with tiny red plums, so sweet and delicious. I don't see their kind anymore. September was also the month for grapes; bittersweet wild grapes grew thick on vines in the woods. Mama put up dozens of jars of grape jam; she also made wonderful savory dumplings that we called grape gudgin. After the first frost, we harvested black haws and persimmons. Orchards provided an abundance of pecans and peaches. The eating was wonderful in fall, a reward for all the hard work we did harvesting and canning. We had to be sure the good eating would take us through winter and its hard times.

Ripening strawberries (to return to spring) signaled the time to plant. Mama laid out long, even rows in the plowed ground. All us kids would walk the rows in our bare feet, stamping in the seeds with our toes. We'd do it first for the potatoes, then repeat the process for the corn and beans and squash and tomatoes and onions and lettuce. Every crop had its moment, and somehow Mama found it. Maybe that was the best trick she learned from Grandma.

Summer began with the last day of school. It was announced by fifty laughing, shouting, skipping children turning cartwheels in the schoolyard. A fine, long, soft summer it was, too, well worth all the noise and tumult.

We had barefoot summers. We had lovely, lazy Huck Finn summers, day upon day of the most glorious freedom. There were grown-ups, certainly. There were chores—more than the rest of the year. We tended the garden, kept a watch for rabbits, hunted birds and jackrabbits, fished, weeded, picked, canned, all that in addition to the washing and cooking and egg gathering that were our share all year round. The chores took three, four hours in days that stretched to fifteen, and beyond fifteen when bonfires lit the night and toasted marshmallows and wieners were the last meal eaten.

The rest of the time, the time beyond labor, we dedicated with single-minded devotion to play. For hour after hour we played at games and sports of our own devising. I've told you about some of them, and I won't repeat. I do want to point out that the decisions between berry picking, cowboys and Indians, high tea in Palm Springs, walking our pipeline high wire, play acting up by the caves, playing with our bear family down by Coon Creek, and splashing and sunning at the swimming hole weren't really ours to make. In a lot of ways, weather made them for us. The fort and the haystacks both became like bake ovens when the hot sun was beating down, so when cloudy and cool came, we jumped at the chance to use them. You had to walk the pipeline when it hadn't rained and you weren't pouring down sweat yourself. Our rock stages up by the cliffs were tolerable in hotter weather. The mud dolls and houses were down by the creek, where we could take splash-off breaks, so those were preferred toys when it got real hot. And when the mercury climbed up around one hundred degrees and over—which it did often enough in high summer—there was nothing to do but go on down to the swimming hole. Of course, there were other factors influencing our decision—who and how many of our playmates were on hand, for one. But that didn't change much. No, it was the weather that chiefly guided our choices.

I want to spend some time on summer specials we haven't talked about yet. For one thing, there was the horse racing that took place almost as regular as church every Sunday. All the kids who had horses—and that was pretty much all the Coon Creek kids—would saddle up, nod solemnly at parental warnings not to race (I've given the same warnings to my girls and accepted the same answers), and trot off to do just that.

We had regular courses mapped out. Some were dirt tracks, and some were cross-country. The races on dirt relied pretty much on the quality of the horses; just about all of us could hang on to a horse, even at full gallop. The cross-country races took us jumping over a lot of bushes and gullies; they called on more from the riders. Old Blackie, the horse I most often rode at these affairs, wasn't blessed with speed. So we competed in the cross-countries. I considered myself a pretty good rider, and the results bore me out. Sometimes I'd come home dirty or even bruised up from the racing. Mama would shake her head but wouldn't say a word about it. I suspect she'd done some racing in her time.

Our play carried on into the night. On Saturdays the Indian families would head on up to Jim Jackson's place for the stomp dances you've heard so much about. Other nights we kids would build big bonfires in the woods, tell tales, roast marshmallows, and play games we wouldn't bring out into the daylight. One of those games we called please or displease. We'd all face the fire, and one of our number would walk around the circle stopping behind each of our backs to ask "please or displease?" Well "pleasing" involved granting requests like kissing your guy (or gal) in front of the group or going off into the woods together. As a group, we were eager to please. I should say that boys and girls paired off pretty young in our part of the country. Not for anything very serious, but everybody knew who went with who. By the time I'd gotten out of grade school, I'd been Percy's girl and Dale's and two, three others' as well.

Summer was the season for festivities. Fourth of July was right up there with Christmas for a special day in our world. There was the Dewey Roundup, which I'll tell you more about in a bit. But that wasn't all. We'd come back after that long, full day to a night of lemonade and fire in the sky. Papa'd bring in fifty pounds of ice to chill down some watermelons and make a big bucket of lemonade. He'd buy five dollars worth of firecrackers in town—you could get a lot of light and noise for five dollars in those days—and he and Henry lit off the rockets and fountains of sparks. What a show.

Summer was the season when circuses and carnivals came to town. There was a stretch of ground down by the tracks; the town had a big tent there. The traveling shows could just unload right from the train and set up, without needing any other hauling equipment. Papa said kids needed excitement, so he took us to every show that passed through. Truth was, he enjoyed the carnivals himself. He'd buy us big bags of peanuts, and we'd leave a trail of shells as we strolled the midway gawking at the sights. Did you ever see a real carnival geek? They had geeks in those old carnivals who absolutely did bite the heads off live chickens. I've seen the hot blood spurt over their faces and the filthy ripped shirts they wore. It was quite a sight. Anyway, we'd be chomping down our cotton candy, spitting out peanuts like it was a hailstorm of shells, and watching the geek do his disgusting thing. After it was all over, we wet down our dry mouths with muscadine punch. That was something they made from muscadine grapes, and it sure was delicious on a hot, dusty carnival afternoon.

We saw family more in summer, too. There was more time for it then. Grammie and Dad Reeve lived in Dewey, and in summer we'd be visiting often. That was especially true of Indie. Indie was the first grandchild and Grammie Reeve's special favorite. Grammie Reeve gave her some wonderful things—ballet lessons and a pretty little pony named Skeeter. She even sent Indie on to college. None of the rest of us got to go, but then things changed a lot between Indie's time and mine. Anyway, the thing is that when she got older, Indie spent a whole lot of her time at the Reeve place in Dewey. She lived there, you might say, and the rest of us would come to visit.

We didn't see nearly as much of the Whiteturkeys. Grandpa lived south of Bartlesville, and it really was an all-day outing to visit him. Of course that made the occasional visits really special. Grandpa Whiteturkey had a birthday party that was a big event on our social calendar. For one thing, it was a gathering of the extended family. All Mama's half-sisters and their husbands and kids came. Grandpa had a big screened outdoor kitchen. The women brought potluck and spent much of the afternoon frying chicken, boiling beans and potatoes, baking cornbread, cooking up catfish the men had pulled out of the river. Grandpa Whiteturkey bought a big three-gallon tub of chocolate ice cream, set it in ice, and just invited us kids to help ourselves whenever we felt like it. We played tag and had races on the lawn; the men threw horseshoes; the women worked. When it came time to eat, the men ate first, then the kids, and women last. But there was always plenty of food to go around.

Autumn added a note of urgency to our lives that was absent the rest of the year. It was the season of new shoes and new teachers. After four glorious months of freedom, we fidgeted under the restraints of our desks and our slates and our shoes. Night fell earlier and earlier, squeezing the time for play, and we lost playmates to the heavy burden of chores. You never knew which game of cowboys and Indians might be the last until spring, so we reveled in each one we were able to play.

Above all, the urgency of autumn lay in the approach of winter. We still lived close enough to the land that winter could be a killing season if we weren't prepared to endure it. There were crops to harvest, fruits and berries to pick, a tremendous amount of canning and preserving to be done. Mama worked without ceasing in the fall, but she couldn't do it all, and we girls hurried home from school to lend a hand. Mostly we relieved her of the mundane chores—washing dishes and clothes, cooking supper, doing simple mending—so she could cure the hams, make the preserves, and put up the hundreds of jars of food we'd devour during the long months of winter dark and chill.

Autumn had its own special releases from the pressure of work. On a clear weekend evening in the fall, we'd get together for a possum hunt. I'm not sure why we picked the fall, since these hunts were conspicuously unsuccessful. But fall was the season established by custom, and fall was the season when we most needed novelty. We'd bring our dogs; we'd all wield big clubs; and contrary to standard hunting practice, we'd make just about as much noise as we could tramping about in the woods at night. I suppose the theory was that our baying dogs and own giggling and shouting would roust the possums from whatever woodland depths they called home. In fact, I think we only encouraged them to climb higher or dig deeper. The neat thing is that when you're really staring into the dark woods, you see all kinds of suggestive shadows and find a hundred different reasons for spine-tingling terror. Possum hunts were so much fun that we continued to hold them even though we never, in my experience, found a single possum.

Fall turned at last to winter. And in the turning there was a danger. The influenza then was deadlier than the influenza now. We lived through the great flu epidemic of 1918; some in our little Coon Creek community did not. I was the last of the Reeve kids to take the flu. I remember, I was standing on a chair to do the dishes. There weren't many dishes; Mama and all my siblings were under quilts in bed, shivering with fever and not exactly ravenous. Papa was beside me; though he was feverish, he took over the care of the family. That's the way he was. I dropped something—I don't know, a spoon maybe—on the floor. Papa put his hand on my forehead and hustled me off to bed. I didn't wash any more dishes for quite a while.

We were lucky in that Papa's sister and my namesake, our dear Aunt Lynn, was a doctor. That meant two things. Papa learned a lot from her, enough to nurse us through the day-to-day aches and sniffles. When we were faced with something more serious, he'd drive over to his folks' place in Dewey, and they'd give Aunt Lynn a call. She had a smart little horse-drawn carriage, and quicker than seemed possible, she'd come prancing up our path to work her healing magic. I don't know just what she did, but Aunt Lynn was a healer. She'd pull out her cold stethoscope and feel around our chest, thumping here and there and having us cough while she listened intently. Then she'd brew up some tea and add one thing or another to it from the pharmacy she carried with her in a big black valise. I've often suspected that some of her medicines weren't so very different from the ones Grandma Wahoney relied on years before. In any case, there was no arguing with her results. Aunt Lynn birthed Mama's babies and persuaded Papa to bring a "har'd girl" into the house for two full weeks following each delivery. She brought all of us through the dread influenza and through the childhood diseases and all the agues and fevers that swept the country. I might not be here today if it weren't for Aunt Lynn's good offices. Thank you, Aunt Lynn.

There was a monotony to the winter months, but also a delicious sort of cozy comfort. The chill and the dark were the two influences that controlled our lives. The cold kept us indoors and, more than that, drew us toward the sources of heat within. We had a fireplace on the first floor and a big woodstove in the kitchen. There was at least one season's difference in temperature between the hot hearts of the house and the walls, where winter seeped in with little serious opposition. The trick was to find the comfort zone, that place between stove and walls where one could live without sweating or shivering, and place table and lamps there. It would have been too easy if that zone remained stationary, but there were many factors that determined its position. Life was not easy.

Snow, when it fell, was a distraction and a delight. We had some terrific snowball fights at school when the yard gleamed white with new snow. We'd take our sleds up to the hills and race them down at dizzying speeds. We'd tromp through the woods in snowshoes. But snow was too often followed by a nasty, stinging drizzle that melted the white as it drove us indoors.

Winter was the season that called on all our ingenuity to use the few resources at hand to fill the time. In the old Indian days, winter was the season for storytelling. We relied on books. Papa was an avid reader who kept our big bookshelf stocked. And we could bring home anything we wanted from the school library. Trouble was, our flickering gas lamps were hard to read by. Eyestrain and headaches developed along with the plot, and sometimes they put a stop to the action. But I still managed to consume a lot of books in those cold winter months, and I've retained my love for reading ever since. Now, in the winter of my life, I find myself once again with time on my hands. And once again I turn to my books for comfort. This time the light is better but the eyes are worse.

Some of the games we relied on back then have pretty much gone out of vogue. The neighbor kids would gather at our place, because Papa was generous and maybe a little overprotective. We'd pull out the dominoes and the checkerboards and go at it. It's amazing how much amusement you can get out of dominoes, where luck is a big part of the game and gives even weak players a chance to win once in a while. It's amazing, too, how good you can get at checkers when you play it over and over. There's some serious strategy to that game, I'll tell you. The trouble is, it got so the same people won every time. I never had any trouble with my pal Ruby, but I couldn't beat my brother Henry to save my life.

One of the games we played back then has gotten more popular with time. We had all kinds of fun when we brought out the decks of cards and played poker. We'd just bet for matchsticks or dry old beans, but that didn't dim our enthusiasm. We mostly played draw poker; even so, we couldn't seem to remember which hand beat which and often had to wake poor Papa to settle arguments about who'd won.

You know, I recently sat down to play some poker with my grandson, and he knew all sorts of games I'd never heard of. I guess things have gotten more complicated at the gaming table since my poker heyday. But there was one game we played that he'd never heard of. We called it nosy poker. The way it went was that instead of betting straws or some such, winners got to sock a loser of their choice in the nose with a full deck of cards. Not too hard, but you didn't want to lose.

It sounds silly. It was. I don't especially want to end our circuit of the year on a silly note. The point is that we weren't afraid to be silly. We had long, dark winters to get through with few resources beyond our mother wit to guide us. We made it to spring every time and always enjoyed the ride.

You know, it really is true that every time you gain something, you lose something else just as important. TV has changed the world, no doubt, and I rely on it myself for entertainment. In those long-ago days, the Coon Creek kids relied on our powers of observation and our imaginations to navigate through time and space. If modern kids have lost that ability, I can't envy them their computers and TVs. Give me nosy poker any time.

Eleven

THE COUNTRY KID
GOES TO TOWN

I grew up a country kid, so that's what I've been telling you about. We'd go weeks at a time entirely enclosed in our comfortable little world, not even thinking about town. But town was there, never far from our reality, shaping us with its distinctive expectations. Dewey was four miles away—long by foot, shorter by horse, next door by car. Bartlesville, big and dynamic, was just five miles farther and linked to Dewey by the interurban. You'd get on that streetcar, and it would shake and roar and the conductor would ring bells at every street and stop. There were spaces on the wire, some kind of connections, where sparks would fly with a kind of popping sound. What a ride that was for a little girl. I've been on carnival rides, roller coasters and such, but nothing ever thrilled me like that trolley.

There was a time, three glorious years, when I got to ride the interurban just about every month. Mama developed some kind of thyroid condition and went to Aunt Lynn for treatment. Every month for about three years she hitched up the horse, took the buggy into Dewey, and caught the streetcar over to Bartlesville, where Aunt Lynn had her office. I was the right age and willing, so I got to be Mama's companion on all these trips to the doctor.

I wasn't keen on sitting in the waiting room, although it did have plush velvet chairs and electric lights, and Aunt Lynn let me pick from a crystal dish filled with saltwater taffy. The sessions took maybe a half hour. I have no idea what went on behind the massive wooden door, but it must have been effective because in time—a long time, yes—Mama got better. But for three years Mama's thyroid put me on that trolley maybe forty times, give or take. I hope the thyroid didn't plague her too much; I'd hate to think I got pleasure through Mama's pain. But pleasure, and an introduction to town life, was mine.

I suppose I thought that life in town was—if you want one word to sum it up—sweet. Well, yes, crowded, noisy, busy, exciting, scary . . . those words came into the picture too. But the one word would have been sweet. Nearly every month, if there wasn't something pressing calling us home, Mama would take me over to the Barlas Ice Cream Parlor. I remember it as a real fancy place—black-and-white tile floor, chandeliers, lots of mirrors, wrought-iron chairs. She went there for the chicken club sandwich that must have been just about her favorite thing to eat. And I got ice cream. Cones, mostly. Sometimes a fountain creation: a soda with balls of ice cream floating in the delicious drink, or a sundae with mounds of chocolate topped by syrup and whipped cream and a maraschino cherry. They made their own ice cream. For me, the Barlas Ice Cream Parlor was the sweet heart of the world. We had some treats back home, but nothing compared to what they served up at Barlas.

I guess I knew that people lived in town. Grammie and Dad Reeve did, and we visited them often enough. We even spent a summer in town, while Papa was off working in Wyoming. We got a place pretty near to the Reeves. We'd drive out to the home place, tend the garden, harvest the crops, and bring them back into town for eating and canning. The best thing about that summer was when it ended and Papa came back to us. He had some pretty good presents with him, Indian things from up

Wyoming way. And he had stories about geysers and pools filled with boiling water. But the best thing was just the way he hugged us, and the look in his eye.

Anyway, as I say, I knew people lived in town. But I guess I really thought that most of the people you saw there were pretty much like us—folks who lived somewhere else and were taking in the sights and excitements. Some Saturday evenings we'd all pile into the Model T, drive on into Dewey, just park on the main drag, and watch the people go by. There was always a throng of people in Dewey on a Saturday night, parading up and down the streets, laughing and talking and having a high old time. It was an entertainment to watch them, to join them in strolling the crowded street, licking an ice cream cone or sipping a lemonade. Better than radio, I promise you. I'd go so far as to say better than TV.

From a very young age, I felt grown up when I went to town. Town meant nice dresses and the cool formality of church. Town was the place where you didn't have to invent your entertainments—they were waiting for you. Town was the place where people were always calling you "young lady." When I was in a town mood, there were things I just wouldn't put up with. Take, for instance, the Easter when I was three. Aunt Shirley and Uncle Joe dropped by to drive us over to Saint Paul's Episcopal for the Easter service. Their boy, Joey, about fourteen and a terrible tease, came along. Now, I was dressed to the nines—Easter bonnet, pink taffeta dress with lacy trim and a big bow that Mama made for the occasion, even frilly little pink panties. I looked great and we were going to town, so I felt on top of the world. Then, for no particular reason except the deviltry of boys of a certain age, Joey put me over his knee, flipped up my skirt, and spanked me on my new panties. It didn't hurt my bottom much, but it offended my dignity so deeply that I started bawling. I told on Joey, loud and long, and he was chastised for his misdeed. But it didn't seem like enough to me. I was three, but I was feeling grown up for the first time in my life, and Joey spoiled it. Come to think of it, maybe he did me a favor. Sometimes, when I get my town dignity up a little too high, I can still feel the sting of his hand on my bottom. It makes it hard to stay haughty.

Town was the place where important people lived, or at least paid a visit. Our little corner of Oklahoma has produced some standouts. The famous Tom Mix was town marshal in Dewey for a brief time, and Gene Autry was discovered in the little train depot at Chelsea, six miles from my current home. But when I was growing up, there was one celebrity in Oklahoma who towered above all the rest. Will Rogers by name. The whole nation knew and loved our Will. With his laid-back humor, his real appreciation for plain folks, his magic with a rope, Will Rogers seemed to sum up everything that was decent and different in our part of the country. His birthday, November 4, was a momentous day in our world. The great man would come back to his home spread, around Claremore, to celebrate with his friends. A big, fine parade wound through the town, with Will Rogers, in his fanciest regalia, riding at the head. Many's the time I've perched on Papa's shoulders just to catch a glimpse of Mr. Will Rogers. My, but he looked fine.

We had some marvelous times in town. Back then, there were circuses and carnivals that made all the rural circuits. Because Bartlesville was flush with oil money, none of them passed us by. And most of those would ride the railroad spur up to Dewey to take advantage of our permanent tent and carnival ground. So we became familiar with an assortment of strongmen and bearded ladies and thrilled to the daring young man on the flying trapeze.

But the best show in town, and the highlight of our calendar, was the annual Dewey Roundup. Every year, the week of July 4, a chunk of Texas, Oklahoma, Kansas, and Arkansas poured into Dewey for the show. The Dewey Roundup was one of the very biggest rodeos anywhere in the U.S.A., as the posters around town proudly proclaimed, and it was the best chance for our local cowpokes to show their stuff. For a week before the start of the Roundup, the most intriguing cast of characters began to assemble in Dewey and neighboring towns. Even along our Coon Creek road we'd begin to get a procession of hard, leathery-looking men on horseback. They were invariably polite, soft-spoken men of few words, but some of them would put on quite a show of fancy riding as they galloped by.

So excitement was in the air, on the roads, building for a week and more before the Roundup kicked on. It built to a fever pitch in the Reeve house, where Papa was not only a calf roper of high repute, a leading figure in the opening day parade, but also one of the Roundup officials, which earned us all free tickets. Papa spent the night in town; the rest of us spent the night in a tizzy. I was up way before the sun, and I'm not sure I was the first one awake. Betty was every bit as eager as I, and even Henry tossed and stirred all night.

I want you to come along with us for a day at the Roundup. We'll be leaving my childhood behind soon enough, but before we do, I invite you to share the joy of one of my best days. It could only have been a town day; it could only have been a day in the twenties, when Oklahoma was flush with oil and fat with cattle; it's a day the likes of which you will never see again.

"Hey." I think I'm the first one up; the bed seems full. It's still dark in the house; I can hardly see in the gloom, but there seems to be a shadow flitting down the stairs. Betty's played a trick on me, piled up pillows so I wouldn't feel her slip off to get to the washbasin first. I don't much mind; truth is, I'm impressed she had her wits about her so early in the morning. But I have to pretend to be mad. "You hoggin' the water, Betty? You always do. You know I hardly use any water washin', and you splash around like an old goose."

"I got a right," Betty snaps back, "same as you. I got up first this time. Anyway, Henry beat us both, is the funny thing. He's dressed already and out workin' his rope."

And so it is, Henry the old sleepyhead has beat us both to the basin. He's out front twirling his lariat and roping stumps. Each year at Roundup time Henry got to admiring Papa's skill as a roper. He wanted to be a rodeo cowboy too and badgered Papa something terrible to show him tricks with the rope. We didn't have any calves to practice on, so Henry roped and tied all the stumps on our place. That's what he's doing in the half light of dawn this morning.

Soon enough Mama's up, bustling about the kitchen, organizing us and the big picnic basket. "Henry, stop that nonsense and hitch up the buggy. Old White Eyes; she won't mind being tied down all day." Mama knows that we're going to eat our way through the day. Of course the ice cream and peanuts and hot dogs are part of the fun, but she doesn't want us to start out ravenous, so she fries up a mess of eggs and potatoes. We're almost too excited to eat, but not quite.

We're hardly the only buggy on the road. Everyone's off to an early start; nobody wants to miss the parade. They've set up a lot of hitching posts in town, but parking the buggy isn't too different from parking your car when there's a big event in town; you have to hunt out a space. By the time we've hitched Old White Eyes up to a post, we have to hurry on down to get a good spot for parade viewing. Mama can walk really fast when she wants to; we string out behind her like ducklings.

I've never seen a parade quite like the one leading off our Dewey Roundup. The street is packed with wranglers riding three abreast; the line of riders stretches up to the grandstand entrance and back down to the rail head and beyond. Every rider is dressed in his snazziest regalia; there are leather vests and chaps, silks of all colors ballooning in the breeze. I don't think anyone looks quite as grand as Papa, but I have to admit that there are some fine-looking cowboys parading by. They're really putting the horses through their paces, too. My, how they prance. There's a fellow bucking and leaping down the street, and another whose golden palomino keeps rearing on its hind legs.

Henry is jumping about like the horses; he's trying to catch a glimpse of Papa in all that throng. At last he cries out, "I see him. There he is." Pretty soon we all see Papa; in his red, white, and blue silks he stands out even in this flashy crowd. Papa's one of the elder statesmen among the rodeo cowboys; he rides Old Brownie at a dignified trot. But when he sees Henry whistling and shouting, he can't resist the impulse to stand up in the saddle and wave his Stetson.

When Papa passes, it's our signal to hurry into the grandstand and find the best seats we can. Mama flashes our passes to the man at the gate. I'm disappointed; I can see we're going to have to sit at the far end. The crowd is even bigger than usual—thousands of people packing the long wooden benches. Henry spots some friends and begs to sit with them; if they squeeze together there'll just be enough room. "Well, you'll miss Grandpa Whiteturkey and his ice cream," Mama reminds him. "We're not gonna come get you." Henry slows down to think it over, then hurries along with us. Grandpa and his ice cream is not something you want to miss.

The first day features preliminaries in nearly all the events. No champions will be crowned for a week, but expert eyes can already pick out likely winners on day one. I'm not that good; I just love to see the ropers and riders. Of course, the bronc and

Brahma bull riding events are the most perilous and exciting. On the first day, when they haven't weeded out the novices and incompetents, a lot of bodies go flying and the rodeo clowns really earn their pay. I've sat a bucking horse a couple of times, so I have some idea how hard that is. I can't even imagine what it takes to sit one of those fierce, muscular Brahmas as it bucks and twists, raising clouds of dust from the dry ground. Most of the bull riders don't seem to have any better idea; they go careening after the first twisting buck. When a rider does hang on to the whistle, we rise as one to applaud.

I can see from the way Henry is staring, eyes bulging and teeth grinding, that he's imagining himself a bull rider. Of course, we're all focusing on the calf roping. Each of us believes Papa can bring home the first prize, although I don't think he harbors any such illusions. But each of us also has a favorite event that captures our imaginations. For Betty it's barrel racing; she's a good rider and longs to race round the barrels herself at one of the Roundups. She doesn't get much encouragement in her ambition from Mama. For Ruth it's steer wrestling. She likes the way those cowboys look when they throw a quarter ton of longhorn steer to the ground. I kind of think she fancies one cowboy in particular, but I'm not sure. I love the bronc riding. If you're really good, you can actually hang on to the whistle. And I can almost feel the thrill of the reins in my hand. Some of the bronc riders have such a flair about them, waving their hats and whooping. By contrast, the bull riders all look scared. But bull riding is the ultimate challenge; no doubt of that. That's what Henry dreams of mastering.

Each of us stares, utterly fascinated, at our favorite event. At other times, eyes wander. We're on the lookout for Grandpa Whiteturkey, whose visits are such a Roundup highlight. You can see him a long way off in his magnificent white Stetson. Of course there are other white hats in the crowd, and some of them fool us in our eagerness. But once Betty spots the oversized white hat, almost like a sailboat on the sea of people, there's no mistaking who it belongs to. Eight eyes stare at the four chocolate cones he carries in a tray above his head. What a great guy; he's actually willing to risk a chocolate drip on his Stetson rather than have someone in the milling throng knock our cones to the ground.

We haven't seen Grandpa in a long time, but after a handshake all round and a few polite words, we're perfectly willing to take his cones and his silver dollars and wander off into the carnival atmosphere surrounding the grandstand. Mama and her dad will talk on into the evening; the cones and money are a kind of bribe to buy some peace and privacy. We'll explore a world of popcorn and cotton candy, of carnival games and kewpie dolls. Henry's a good enough shot to win a prize with the rifle; he fires off a dead-eye shot, then hurries to check on our buggy and the patient Old White Eyes. Today I'm lucky enough to knock over three bottles with a single ball toss and walk away with a teddy bear for a prize. I don't usually win much, so I'm eager to show off. I'm on the lookout for Ruby Wittenburg, and I finally spot her. "Hey, Ruby," I shout across the crowded fairgrounds, jumping up and down to get her attention. She sees me. It turns out she's won something too, a sparkly little windmill. We both agree that my prize is tops. Since I still have the better part of Grandpa Whiteturkey's dollar, I buy us both a cup of muscadine punch. Boy is that punch good; nothing cuts through the dust in your throat quite like that cold grape drink. Then we head over to the animal pens.

Lots of kids have gathered by the wooden fences. This is where all the stock is penned — the big, raw mustangs with that wild look in their eyes; the longhorn steers with those sweeping swords on their heads; the calves, nimble and spooky; the cow ponies with their soft, wise eyes; and of course the Brahma bulls. Henry's over by the bull yard, and we join him. I have to admit the bulls are a sight. They're unbelievably massive up close. Their muscular shoulders and their great humps ripple in a casual display of power when the flies plague them. Mostly the bulls are at rest, at ease, contemptuous of us. Once in a while one will stand up and shudder the fence with a casual jolt. How fragile the massive old timbers look then; we instinctively shrink back from the display of raw power. But in truth the bulls are placid beasts except when some fool annoys them by jumping on their backs; they have no interest in shattering the fence.

The emcee is bellowing through his big bullhorn for the calf ropers to take their places. That's our signal to hurry back to Mama's side. There's maybe twenty ropers in all; a half dozen hold themselves in the saddle in a way that tells us they're serious competitors. Papa's one of the oldest; among these thousands of onlookers, we're probably the only ones who think he has a real chance. I'm getting tense waiting for Papa to take his turn; from the way Betty squeezes my hand, I know just how excited she is. At last Papa lines up beside the chute; the gate opens; the calf bolts; Papa's on him in an instant, lariat twirling; now the calf's on its back and Papa has his rope around three legs. It's only taken a couple of seconds. Papa doffs his hat to thunderous applause. He may not end up with the first prize, but he's posted the best time today.

Night falls. The official festivities draw to a close. The trickle of riders and buggies leaving town on every road becomes a torrent. Satisfied, tired, happy, the Reeve family is among them. We'll sleep well tonight; our sleep will be blessed with sweet dreams.

I knew in the living of it that it had been a great day.

I wouldn't realize for many years how very close to perfect these best days of my childhood truly were, how terribly difficult it would be to reclaim the joy in the moment, the comfort of friendship, that came so naturally then. Maybe those of us who have been blessed in childhood with love and comfort, with family and friendship and the freedom to play, with honored traditions and ceremonies, spend our adult lives in search of the same. I know I've done that, and I thank God, my Delaware people, and Mama and Papa that I had a childhood that encouraged me to do it.

Childhood's
End

Twelve

TOUCHED BY HISTORY

For the first fourteen years of my life, it seemed we lived in some sort of rural Eden. The world couldn't touch us; if we read the newspaper, it was to see what was happening "out there" in a big world that seemed so far away. And then, without warning, history found us out in our Coon Creek hideaway, picked us up by the scruff of the neck, and shook my childhood away.

The Bible tells us that when history begins, paradise ends. That's deep, and I'm not sure about it as a general proposition, but it seems to fit my life pretty well. Within just a few years of the crash of '29, my family had scattered, our rural community had emptied, I had begun life on very different terms as an adult.

To put it another way, I suppose a simpler way, our world—and not just Grandma's dolls—was buried by an irresistible tide of events in just a few years of the thirties. I guess I never could accept that. I've spent much of my adult life trying to reclaim the comforts of family and community that I lost so suddenly. Trying, if you will, to bring the Delaware dolls and so much else back to light. That really is the major theme of the second part of my story—how, with support from my husband, my family, my church, my community—I did regain at Winganon so much of what I treasured at Coon Creek.

I don't want you to think for a minute that I literally dug up Grandma's dolls; they're with her in the ground for eternity. What I actually did was far more satisfying to me. But I don't want to get ahead of my story; now is the time to take a hard look at the end of innocence for the Reeves.

History descended upon us as the Great Depression, which struck Oklahoma in the particularly virulent form known as the Dust Bowl. John Steinbeck is the scribe of that saga, and I'm not going to compete with him in the telling. I will cite you a few instances of how the bad times took the Reeves and turned us upside down.

First of all, I should say that the drying and blowing away of the farmland really took place west of us. We were dry; the crops were down; it got harder to coax a harvest out of our fertile soil. Coon Creek came near to drying up in the heat of summer, and we had to haul more water barrels up to the deep well and back than ever before. There were days when clouds of dust dulled the sun to a dim copper and laid a layer of fine powder over the face of Mother Earth that did not improve her looks. We knew it was good farmland, belonging to people like us who just happened to live a few hundred miles west, that was falling on our heads. Knowing that just made us feel mournful.

For all that, Mama's garden held up. It was good that it did; more than ever, the beans and corn and squash and tomatoes and poultry and eggs we produced at home were what kept body and soul together. What didn't hold up was the money. The oil business was hard hit by the bad times, and Papa's salary from maintaining pumps and pipelines was slashed to something like thirty-five dollars a month. We were never self-sufficient and always needed to supplement what we grew with store-bought goods. Now it was so hard to get cash money that we all had to devote ourselves to it. There wasn't time anymore for the hunting and trapping and fishing that had provided such a nice addition to our table.

The effects of the depression on the Reeve family:

We lost our car first, then our buggy; they were luxuries we couldn't afford in those dire times. Mama had to walk the four miles to Dewey to get groceries. She'd come back from that long trek, arms loaded with bags of food and necessities, looking just as composed as when she left. She was one strong lady, was Mama. But there were times I saw her up the hill a piece, her head in her hands, despairing. No individual is stronger than the world.

Before the depression, Indie went on to college and Ruth graduated from high school. Caught in its grip, Henry and I both dropped out of high school. There wasn't enough money for the clothes and shoes and other necessities. The four-mile walk to Dewey, the constant embarrassments — it all got to be too much. And there was work to be done. Henry rode the rails looking for it; I found it closer to home.

Papa did the best he could to keep me in school clothes; I know he sacrificed so I could carry on. One memory embarrasses me now, when I think back on it. It was a hard winter, and Papa bought me a pair of arctics. They were clunky, high, fur-topped boots that kept out every hint of the cold. I know he couldn't really afford them. Trouble was, he didn't consult me about them, and they were eyesores. Nobody else in school wore anything like them, and I wasn't secure enough to be a trendsetter. So what I did was make a little detour on the way to school and hide those arctics under a neighbor's porch; then I'd return them to my feet on the way home. Can you imagine? It would have hurt Papa so to know how I treated his loving gesture, but high-school girls are what they are.

Ruth had married and left our home place a few years before. She lived in Dewey with her husband, Dick Alton, and a growing family on its way to numbering three kids. They occupied a few rooms above the bakery that was the Alton family business. Dick and Ruth ran the business, baking the breads and cookies and pretty iced cakes and dealing with the public. That and raising a family proved to be a burden on Ruth. She needed help, and I was there to give it. I spent more and more time living with the sister I loved best, helping her struggle through. She'd watch the store, I'd watch the kids; I'd watch the store, she'd . . . you get the idea. Both of us would get up about 5 A.M., while the babies slept, and creep downstairs to ice the tea cakes. I'd whip up a batch of white icing and spread it on; Ruth would follow along squeezing on little pink roses. Those tea cakes looked wonderful and tasted yummy; they were a great favorite with the public. When we finished; we'd slip back upstairs and grab another hour's sleep.

I was important to Ruth; I liked the work; school seemed more and more irrelevant. I dropped out of high school in the eleventh grade and only felt bad about it years later.

The depression shook the confidence of Mama and Papa. As far as I can remember, it was the first time they came up against problems that were too big for them. They couldn't keep up the car, or even feed all the horses. They couldn't keep all the kids in school clothes. Our education, which was so important to them, was suffering. Come evening, so many evenings, they would walk off together, out of earshot, and huddle in sad, serious talk.

At the same time, depression or no, Indie and Delmar Sanders were beginning to do pretty well down in Beaumont, Texas. His law practice flourished; they began to acquire money and power, making their way in a society far more worldly than anything I've been comfortable with. They sent us a seductive message: Come on down here, life is good here. We can get you good jobs here. Their motives were generous, I know. They meant the best for us. Ruth and Dick heeded their call. To my great surprise, so did

Mama and Papa. As it turned out, they were happy enough down in Beaumont; it was good for them.

To me, it was stunning to see my family splinter, one after the other drifting on down to Beaumont or to other, more distant, ports of call. I'd always believed they valued our home place just as I did. I didn't share the ambitions that made Texas attractive to them. I was happy where I was and didn't want to join them. But I don't know if I would have had the strength to hold out on my own. I've always thought of Indie and Ruth as being stronger, more capable than I could hope to be. When I was a child, I often did what they told me. Now they were telling me to come on down to Texas. With the both of them urging me on, I might have ended up in Beaumont too. I needed something to hold on to, someone who was strong enough to support my determination to live in the land I loved.

Thirteen

GORDON PERRY

I found my partner, my strength, the love of my life in high school, lost him for a time, then found him again and never let him go.

Gordon B. Perry was the man I would love and share my life with for forty-five years. He was a good-looking young fellow, was Gordon, and I won't pretend that wasn't important to me. In a few years he would look quite a bit like Gary Cooper. I'm not the only one who's said so, not by a long shot. He hadn't grown into that look yet in high school, but he was already straight and strong, with bright, piercing eyes and a kind, knowing smile. He was a quiet fellow, a man of few words all his life, but he also had a sly sense of humor that you didn't see coming until it had already come, if you know what I mean.

We met at a skating party at the local community center. I was starting high school, and I guess I caught a few eyes. Anyway, boys were talking to me all night; I was a center of attention. When it came time to walk home, I was besieged by boys wanting to escort me. Out of that crowd, I picked Gordon. For me it wasn't a tough choice; he was the clear standout.

Some years later we shared a silly little intimacy that somehow brought us closer together. I was walking, and Gordon caught up to me. He started teasing me, in a flirty kind of way, about how I was only a freshman and he was a senior. I had to correct him, reminding him that I was in fact a junior, just about his own age. He was finishing up a candy bar, and I allowed as how I would like one myself. He denied that he had any, but I spotted a suspicious bulge in the back pocket of his loose-fitting overalls. Bolder than I can quite explain, I reached my hand in. "Here's another," I proudly proclaimed, fishing a jockstrap out of his pocket. I wasn't quite sure what it was, but I knew it was nasty, and I dropped it with a shriek. Flushing deep shades of crimson, Gordon picked it up and ran off. We spoke no more that day, but somehow the awkwardness of that moment ended our shyness. Ice had been broken.

I should say that Gordon didn't often blush, but that silly incident turned him crimson one more time. What happened was this: Some years after we married, I entered a jingle contest held by a local radio personality named Sam Snyder and won two hundred dollars for placing second. It was money we used to purchase the Hereford calf that founded our herd. Anyway, part of the prize was appearing on a live interview on the Snyder show. We talked about one thing and another, and finally he got around to asking me how I met my husband. I knew Gordon would be listening, so I launched into the candy bar story, coming perilously close to the part about the jockstrap. Only, in my telling there was a candy bar in his pocket. Later Gordon's sister Maisel, who'd been listening with him, told me his face had turned many shades of red. I wish I could have seen it.

Pretty soon we were an item, going to all the school dances together. Times were hard; a date might involve a visit to the ice cream parlor to sip a soda from two straws. That wasn't important; I just liked being with Gordon. For one thing, it was flattering to have a boy who was widely considered one of the best-looking in the school as my beau. What's more, Gordon was held to be something of a ladies' man, and all the girls were jealous. But it wasn't just that; there was a quiet strength about him that I felt I could lean on. And I did lean on it, for much of my life.

Right after graduating, Gordon left town to find work at a CCC camp. For three years he lived in a barracks near Battiest, a little town in the rugged mountains of southern Oklahoma. He labored at backbreaking work clearing timber and building roads through the mountains for thirty dollars a month, twenty-five of which he sent home to support his family during the hard times. The food couldn't have been any too good; Gordon was painfully thin when next I saw him. But he got through it.

Out of love and loneliness, Gordon wrote me some wonderful letters that I keep and treasure to this day. But three years is a long time in the lives of young people. The letters stopped. Gordon met other girls; I got to know other boys. When Gordon returned from the CCC camp, it wasn't to run into my arms.

As it happened, we were both living around Nowata, a little town thirty miles east of Dewey, and God, I believe, put us in each other's path from time to time. If there are marriages made in heaven, I claim ours was one. For all that, though, it was not a big or particularly festive wedding. In 1940, after ten years of struggle just to put food on the table, most people in our part of the country got married pretty much the way we did—modestly, in a little rural church, in the company of a few close friends and family members.

Gordon got himself a job with Forest Oil just about a week after we got married and not long after I started as a file clerk at City Service Gas. It was at this job that Gordon learned what would become his life's work. Starting as a welder's assistant, and working for a man who did not want him to learn the trade, Gordon studied every move his boss made and soon picked up what he needed to know.

This may seem like a strange thing to say, but even in high school Gordon was a son of Oklahoma, and I loved that in him. Let me explain. As a welder, he healed rips and wounds in the pipelines and gas tanks that hold and carry our state's number one product—crude oil and refined gasoline. That's a difficult and delicate and dangerous job, welding the tanks; not many will do it. If they're not washed clean, if even a little residue of gas remains in those big smelly tanks, they'll blow sky high as soon as you light up that torch. It's happened plenty of times. Gordon was a careful man. He knew the risks, and he took pains to minimize them. He supervised every step of the cleaning. He examined every crevice and joint. His supervisors were always urging speed, but he ignored them. They didn't have the nerve to step into those tanks and turn on the flame, and he knew it.

That's another way Gordon was a true son of Oklahoma: he had a stiff back. I mean that physically—his job involved a lot of stooping and bending over pipes and tank floors, and he'd come home in agony with his back seizing up. I also mean it spiritually—Gordon didn't bow or scrape to anyone. He worked a dangerous job, I believe, because it gave him the freedom to work on his own terms. When he welded fence for a neighbor, it was Gordon who found the best line—the shortest and straightest. On our spread, at the fishing hole, among his friends, Gordon was always his own man. That's a rare thing; I like to think it's a point of country pride, of Oklahoma pride.

Gordon also knew cattle, Oklahoma's second product. Every evening he'd call in our cows, and there was a tone in his voice that brooked no disobedience. They came. He could smack our bull on the snout with a stout stick, and the brute would fall in line. He got cows through their calving, nursed the sick back to health. We never had a big herd, but Gordon could have handled one; no question.

Gordon was comfortable with the Indian side of Oklahoma. He understood my need to take part in some of the dances and feasts the tribes put on; I think he enjoyed it all almost as much as I did. The Shawnee people held a Bread Dance west of White Oak; it had been going on for a long, long time. The season was fall; I believe it had something to do with the Green Corn ceremony, the great harvest feast of some of the eastern tribes. It went on for days, people visiting and dancing round a big old fire in a clearing in the woods. Some of them camped out there for the whole run; Gordon and I and lots of others came for just one evening, sat on the rows of log benches, ate Indian food and talked to old friends, and now and then joined the dance. We danced in ordinary clothes, none of the fancy costumes you see at powwows these days. Gordon was welcome to dance; everyone who came was welcome. He didn't do it often, but that wasn't the point; that he was welcome was what counted. It was just the same at the Copan powwow, started by the famous Delaware George Fall Leaf and carried on by the family. It's a funny thing, I didn't go as a child, with Mama and Papa. Only started after I met Gordon. I've been circling the Delaware side all my life; sometimes when it seemed I was moving away, I was also moving toward.

Gordon was a self-reliant man. There was nothing on the farm he couldn't fix, nothing I needed that he didn't improvise, no problem he wouldn't take on. To sum it up: Gordon was a rock; he loved the land; he was an honorable man who did his work with pride; he could be narrow-minded, I guess; what he knew contented him, and he knew Oklahoma top to bottom; what he didn't know he didn't much care about.

In his virtues and his vices, Gordon was a son of this land, an Oklahoman. I keep coming back to that because it was so very important to me.

You see, Mama and Papa heeded the call to move down to Texas. By this time it seemed that Beaumont was becoming the new Reeve home place. But it didn't feel like home to me. My brother-in-law was moving up the ladder in Texas politics and acquiring property along the way. There was a lot about that I didn't understand, a lot I didn't want to understand. My sister Indie was acquiring airs along with her new social status—she'd have said "manners," and you might well agree with her judgment about it. But when Gordon and I came down for our occasional visits, there just wasn't much doubt about who the country cousins were.

Gordon would have none of that. He had no patience with people who thought they were better. As far as he was concerned, no one was better than we were; and in that I tend to agree.

Gordon was suited to Oklahoma; it's hard to imagine him living anywhere else. I was suited to Oklahoma; I knew I'd never find my rightful home any other place. So we stayed pretty near to where we were born and made our lives there.

Fourteen

WE FIND OUR
HOME PLACE

It's a truism that the older you get, the faster time seems to pass. When I was a girl, those long, lovely summers went on and on. Now years slip by faster than a single summer did then. Maybe that's part of the reason I wanted children so much; I hoped they'd bring some of those endless summer days back into my life. You know, they did that, too, as far as such things are possible.

Gordon and I were terribly disappointed to find that we couldn't have children of our own. That didn't deter us; it just changed our schedule a little. We made ready to invite someone else's child into our lives.

Before we could do that, we had to be able to provide a physical home and a spiritual home. I believe that down to my bones. I think that strong, strong feelings about home and family make up the common ground between the two cultures that have shaped me—Delaware and Oklahoma Baptist. For both, a home is so much more than a structure, a shelter. Home is the place where the people and spiritual forces that nurture you come together. We spent a good many years preparing the homes our children could share with us.

It took us a deal of moving around to find the little community of Winganon, not even a dot on the map, that would provide home for body and spirit. We were restless perhaps, or simply

caught up in our struggle to escape poverty. We moved again and
again, short moves in the oil and cattle country between Dewey
and the Verdigris River, thirty miles to the south. The places
we stayed in all had two things in common: they were bargain
basement, and nobody could mistake them for home. It got so
that Hap Greenberg, the mailman for our sparsely populated
district, greeted one of our moves with this request: "I wish you
kids would start paying your rent so you could stay in the same
place for a year or so."

We did pay our rent, and we always made sure to live in a place
where rent was cheap enough that we could put a little money
away. Always building that nest egg; holding on to the dream
Gordon and I shared of a place and time where we could bring
children into our lives

As it turned out, we found a spiritual home first, and that led
us to our dwelling place. The home I'm talking about wasn't as
grand to look at as Saint Paul's Episcopal Church. It was a trim
country church, the Winganon Baptist Church, that anchored
a cluster of houses, a store and school, and little more. It was a
modest house of worship, but glorious to me, because the Lord
dwelled within its walls. I should say that he dwelled there for me,
as he did not in Saint Paul's. Mama found him in Saint Paul's,
I'm sure of that. He is to be found in all of the many, many houses
built in his honor, and in countless other places as well. But not
everywhere for everyone. I enjoyed the services at Saint Paul's
sometimes and found it an impressive place always, but I don't
think I was serious about religion then.

I once made a mistake, amusing but also revealing. Gordon's
people were Baptist, and his sisters were earnest about it. I went
to church one Sunday with his sister Gladys; after the service
we stopped for a minute to chat with the preacher. "Are you
a Christian?" he asked me, by which I now know he meant to

ask whether I'd accepted Jesus as my personal savior. A little flustered, I answered, "No, I'm Episcopalian." I'm sure I gave him a laugh and a story he could use at meetings of the Baptist convention. But in a way I was expressing a deeper confusion. I was Episcopalian, yes, but I wasn't really much of a Christian. I hadn't read the Bible through or carefully. I was confused about what I believed, about the role of Christ in my life.

Now, Gordon's people were by no means the only Baptists hereabouts. Most of our neighbors and friends—the majority, certainly—belonged to one or another Baptist congregation. A lot of the tiny communities dotting the countryside were built around a Baptist church. Baptist preachers were the counselors and sages of our country. My friends would talk to me about church, how it was the center of their community and all sorts of interesting activities. That I could understand and appreciate. They'd talk to me about accepting Jesus Christ as my personal savior. That I didn't really understand; it made me a little nervous.

A couple of my friends, Birdie and Catherine, invited me up to a revival with their church, the Winganon Baptist Church. I wasn't sure about it, but something told me I was ready to take a closer look at what this was all about. I said yes, I'd go with them. I don't know, maybe I was a little anxious about it, on edge. Anyway, I sat out in a chair, turned on the radio. Fred Waring was playing Easter music, beautiful music. I closed my eyes and just let the music wash over me, almost like the waters of baptism. I felt completely at peace; there was nothing but that music and the warm kiss of the sun in all the world, no room for questions or doubts. Then, suddenly, there was something else in the world, in my heart. I felt the presence of the Lord: personal, thrilling, profound. The Lord was all around me, offering me his unconditional love. All I had to do was accept his gift, to let him into my heart. I knew this was real, more real than anything that had ever happened to me before. And I knew, absolutely, that all my sins would be forgiven, my questions answered, my doubts and fears banished. I would find my peace.

The weekend of the revival passed like a dream. People were gracious, accepting, knowing. Clearly, many of them had been through something like this themselves. I felt special, and I wanted to hang onto that feeling. I didn't want to share it or to talk. They seemed to understand that and to give me my space. We did agree that I would come to church the next Sunday and do whatever felt right.

I asked Gordon to come to church with me. He didn't go often, but this time he said yes. We sat near the back, on one of the hard benches. The minister asked for all the people who had accepted Christ into their hearts to come forward. Several people rose; I stood up with them. The minister shook my hand and welcomed me; nearly everyone in the congregation did the same. I felt at ease. I felt at home.

I was baptized, along with four others, in the waters of Spencer Creek. I immersed my body in the water and rose up, feeling refreshed and reborn. I will tell you that while the solemn ceremony was proceeding, a number of pigs swam and splashed in the same creek, some way above. I don't know what that might have meant; maybe that all of nature is holy, or maybe that we shouldn't ever lose our sense of humor. Maybe both.

I was welcomed into the community of the Winganon Baptist Church by Shug and Birdie and Kate—women who would be friends and soul mates all my life. Let me say this just as clearly as I can: Church has been the most important element in my adult life. It has been community for me. It has provided the members of what I like to think of as my extended family. It has filled my days with purpose.

Church opened up all sorts of fascinating interests and activities. There were picnics and potluck dinners; we got together a couple of times a week. There was Bible school for the young ones and Bible camp in the summer. We had a Women's Missionary Union that supported the missionary work around the world. We'd get some fascinating speakers to come and tell us about the good work being done in exotic places. They'd show us movies sometimes, travelogues. A speaker who'd actually done the Lord's work in the Congo or along the Amazon would take us landlocked Oklahoma ladies over the water and far away with her words and pictures. I've always wanted to know all I could about the world, had a yen to travel. So I've watched movies and TV shows about places like Egypt and Japan whenever I could. But nothing captured my interest like those missionary lectures. Sometimes I even dreamed of joining the missions myself.

Most of the good works our church community performs are much closer to home. We are our brother's keepers. If someone takes bad sick, we make sure to bring over good home-cooked meals, even take in the kids if need be. And when someone dies, the whole countryside rallies round. Everyone will bring a big casserole dish or stewpot or cake or loaf of fresh-baked bread or pitcher of lemonade. No one plans it; it's as if there's an instinct of goodness in the land. The people I live with can be mighty fine, especially when it comes to looking out for one another.

Right after I joined the congregation, our preacher assigned me to teach Bible class to some very bright fourteen- and fifteen-year-olds. Now, I really hadn't studied the book; I was a long way from knowing it chapter and verse. Truth to tell, many of these young people, who'd been going to Bible class since they were babies, knew the Scriptures better than I did. I read, I studied, I tried to keep at least a little ahead of my class. Together we worked our way through the book; for the first few years, they probably taught me more than I taught them.

I want to clear up a misconception. A lot of people, too many people in America, believe that because Baptists, fundamentalists, take the Bible literally, we don't really think about our religion. I'm here to tell you that we're just as thoughtful and earnest about Scripture as we can be. A Baptist minister might have a tiny congregation, fifty people in a humble rural church, but he'll do everything in his power to lead that small flock to God's truth.

The thing I like most about the Baptist approach to the faith is that it takes the Bible seriously, takes the Lord seriously. We believe that every passage in the book is a communication from God, a truth that we have a duty to take into our hearts, to understand.

I don't think too many of us take anything seriously anymore. What, sports? The O. J. Simpson trial? The things that fascinate people these days don't really reward their attention. I know people who debated every piece of evidence in the Simpson trial. What for? What did it mean to them? I'm so grateful to the church for giving me ideas and questions to be serious about that do reward my effort. As we read through the book with the minister as our guide, we talk about the message, try to work our way to understanding just what it is, what it's telling us about how to live our lives. It can be an urgent and stimulating process. It can be the most intense struggle to think and understand I've ever experienced. I appreciate many things about the church, most of all the chance to think hard about important matters. Without that, what's the point?

I've wondered lately whether other religions can offer the pleasure that means so much to me, whether they too can reveal truth. When Grandma Wahoney danced and chanted in the Big

House, was she leading her people to the heart of her story? Was she teaching them what I would call a lesson in salvation—that God loves the little children? I don't know if I'll ever be sure about that. I believe that my Delaware ancestors worshiped the same God I do, in a manner that he found pleasing in that time and place.

But what I know, without question, is that my own faith offers the one certain path to salvation in this time and place. I've wondered what it might have been like to be a Delaware in the Big House. I don't consider it a loss in any way that I'll never know. The truth that I do know is the greatest truth, God's ultimate gift to his people. I am a Christian; I believe that Christ died for our sins, and that his gift of grace is the only sure path to salvation. I am grateful for that gift, and I would never put it at risk.

So if you were to ask me, would I visit the Big House and take part in the Gamwing ceremony if I could, I'd have to tell you no. I'm fascinated by it; I would love to observe it. But I wouldn't take part. My Christian worship delights me; it is enough. I know that the devil works in devious ways; I'm afraid that he may occupy the empty houses where God once dwelled. God no longer visits the Big House; I believe that he has moved on to his churches. If I were to worship in the Big House now, I'm not so sure who I would find there.

We wanted our own house, the place where we would raise our children, to be a house dear to God. So as soon as we could, Gordon and I moved close to our new community, our new friends. We took our savings and bought an eighty-acre spread almost adjacent to the church. We had a neat little house built, just a couple of rooms, but enough. I tried to put in a garden, like Mama, but there were a couple of horses that strayed over the countryside and ate my crops as they poked out of the ground. So we fenced in the place. Gordon, being a welder, knew how to put up fence. He'd secure a post, we'd run the roll of barbed wire over to it, he'd weld the wire on. It didn't take too long, really, to fence in the whole eighty acres.

We were comfortable, happy, convinced we'd found our home. Then we met Jack Cochran and really did find it. Jack was an old rancher and farmer, too old to run his spread anymore. He lived with his niece and her family when I met him; their place wasn't more than a half mile south of ours. I wanted to pick up some rocks I'd spotted along his driveway, and I was a little curious about the old man who never came to church and was much gossiped about. I found him to be a nice enough old fellow, somewhat lonely and worried about the future because his niece and her family were preparing to move away. I thought it was my Christian duty to look in on Jack, and it gave me something to do. Pretty soon I found myself driving him to town from time to time, where he liked to buy himself an ice cream and watch the people walk by.

One day Jack came over to our place and asked Gordon and me to move into his home and take care of him. If we did, he said, he'd leave us the house and 160-acre spread when he died. Well, we were quite content where we lived and told him no. Then, when I brought over something I'd cooked for Jack, I found that he'd had a lawyer draw him up a contract. The essence of it was that we'd move in and take care of him, treat him as family, nurse him through his last illness, and when he died the place would become ours. He wanted to handle it as a contract instead of a will so there wouldn't be any delays.

We talked it over, prayed about it, and decided that it would be a blessing for both parties. So we moved in with Jack and, as it developed, lived with him for three years. He turned out to be a pretty easygoing old fellow, not hard to cook for, tough and uncomplaining. He had some friends, old drinking buddies and such, who would drop over from time to time, but not too often. He had an old cot that he'd put out in front, where he could watch the cars pass up and down our road. He was easily entertained, really.

There were some things he wanted to do that I helped him with. Together we planted a big strawberry patch that took hold and produced some luscious berries until a drought killed it a few years later. Jack helped me tend our chickens. Gordon cared for his cattle — he had about thirty head, and he was the one who sold me the two-hundred-dollar Hereford that founded our herd. I like to think I was helpful to Jack in another way as well. He wasn't a churchgoing man, but we had long talks about Christ and salvation, and I think Jack began to see the light. He came to church with me from time to time, and I know he took to praying. He never was baptized — he'd gotten sick and weak by then — but I believe he was saved at the end.

The first time Jack took sick, we brought him in to the hospital, which was the standard thing to do. Jack wasn't used to such treatment, though, and when he came back he said he'd rather be hung with a wet rope than go back there again. So when he entered his final illness, I pretty much had the care of him. Our regular doctor came out from time to time to guide me through it, but there wasn't anything medicine could do except suggest ways to make Jack more comfortable. The nursing grew to be a full-time job, really a difficult and demanding process. We set up foam rubber pads on his bed so he wouldn't get bedsores. It got so he couldn't eat and was so weak that I had to bathe him in bed and change his position. There were bedpans and enemas. Sometimes the women from church would come around to "help," but they weren't used to the procedure and found it kind of overwhelming. I'd find myself with two patients to care for when a "helper" got a little hysterical on me.

For about a year, Jack's sickness and need filled my life. I have to tell you that I didn't mind feeling needed and useful; Gordon could be pretty independent. Nursing Jack was something that suited me; I have wondered from time to time whether I should have gone to school and gotten the training I needed to become a hospital nurse.

In a way this was my missionary work, without the foreign culture and exotic locale. And, like a good missionary, I could feel some real satisfaction at the result. You see, Jack had a vision just before he died. He looked straight up and said "Letty." Letty was the name of his deceased wife; I believe he saw her at the end. Then he said "Mama." And finally "Jesus." I believe that Jack died with a vision of Jesus in his heart, and that he did go to his reward.

We buried Jack with full ceremony. The whole church came together to bid him farewell and to comfort us; he'd truly become a member of the family. Then we moved our remaining possessions up into his house, which had become ours, and rented out the place below. The house was an old one, lacking in many comforts and without indoor plumbing or running water, but it was warm and cozy and very livable. I'd been devoting all my time to caring for Jack, and I found myself with time on my hands and a need to give and receive love. It was time for the Perrys to find our family.

Hellos and
Good-byes

Fifteen

MEETING OUR CHILDREN

I look at my life from the mountaintop of old age and see how important family—all the variations of family that have filled my years with purpose and joy—truly has been.

Gordon and I were ready to find our children. I want to tell the kids about that as I tell you; things that I myself didn't know until I started to think about them now, for this. There are motives you recognize at the time, and there are reasons you only understand years later.

When Jack Cochran died, I found that my need to be needed was maybe greater than ever. I wanted children more urgently than before; I thought we were now in a position to welcome them. Gordon and I had talked about adopting for years; we both felt this was the time to act.

We wanted a baby. We expected to adopt one baby. A girl. But I wanted her to be an Indian child. I needed her to be an Indian child. I didn't know why at the time, but it was such a strong feeling I never questioned it. Gordon understood me, maybe better than I understood myself, and agreed to my wish.

What I think now is that with my family moving down to Beaumont, out to California, I felt I was losing something. I was in danger of losing touch with my Indian side, if I can put it that way. Gordon had a big family, and they were all around. I got to know them, enjoyed them mostly; Gordon's sister Maisel became a great friend and wonderful traveling companion. But there were Perrys all over eastern Oklahoma and western Arkansas, and I guess I felt a little like an outsider. I worshiped in Gordon's church and felt at home there—more at home than ever at Saint Paul's Episcopal—and yet I was a newcomer there too. My new world was good, but I needed to connect it to the world I grew up in, a world I still valued enormously.

I guess, when you get down to it, I needed to get back in touch with a part of me that meant more than I generally let myself know. The Delaware part. Somehow I thought that adopting an Indian child would do that for me, would make my life whole. I didn't understand that back then, couldn't have put it into words at all. Gordon put up no resistance to the idea, which was a little strange, because there were those in our part of the country—and in his big clan—who believed down deep that Indians weren't as good as lighter-skinned folks. So maybe he did understand where I was coming from better than I did myself. I don't know; we really didn't talk about those kind of feelings too much.

Anyway, it turned out that adopting an Indian child was more complicated and limiting than we expected. Gordon and I went down to Vinita, just twenty miles east, and filled out all the forms for the Department of Human Services, or whatever, but they had no Indian babies, and no clear prospects for getting any.

When you've set your heart on something, it's hard to take "indefinite wait" for an answer. Gordon and I put out feelers. We asked our friends at church, our preacher. It turned out that Katie, one of our regulars, had a sister who worked down in Muskogee at Bacone College. She told us about the Indian orphanage down there. Our preacher, Steve Cleamons, interceded on our behalf with Reverend Roe Beard of Muskogee. I don't know why I give you the lineage, except to show that I remember it all so many years later. It was the most important thing in my life then; I jumped to the phone hoping for news, for progress.

The upshot of all our effort was that I rang up Mrs. Alice B. Joseph at the Murrow Indian Orphanage. Miss Joe, as her charges called her, brooked no nonsense. I'm something of a no-nonsense girl myself, so we hit it off pretty well. I wasn't so happy to hear that they took in no one younger than seven, but when she invited me to come down and meet some of the little orphans, I decided to take her up on it.

I don't remember most of the kids I met. The ones who stuck in my mind then, and to this day, were the little Lakoe girls, ten-year-old Linda and eight-year-old Jackie (not her real name, but I'll go along with Linda in using it). They were little Apache girls, full-bloods to look at them, with fierce black eyes. Jackie was plump and adorable, and she knew it. She knew how to use it, too! I could see her working on me right away from that first meeting. She made it very clear that she desperately wanted to be adopted, and I felt half inclined to oblige her. But I wasn't eager to split up two sisters who'd traveled so far together. Miss Joe soon gave me to know that the law wouldn't allow me to do it, either. Those two girls were bound together by court order. You adopted both or neither. No ifs, ands, or buts.

It was easy to see that Linda would pose the greater challenge. She was cool; she was withdrawn; she had a way of sizing you up with a look. She was going to reserve judgment until she had a chance to make up her mind, and she'd do it in her own time. Miss Joe seemed to have a quiet affection, maybe even admiration, for Linda. She told me about a school art contest in Muskogee where Linda took an honorable mention. She allowed as how she really thought the drawing was worth a blue ribbon. Now, maybe she was trying to impress me; I considered that. But when Linda drew me a fabulous blue bird—more like a peacock than any blue bird I've ever seen—I could tell she had talent. I've always had an interest in art, and Gordon didn't really understand what that was all about. So the idea of having a child who might have some sympathy with that side of me—I have to tell you that was appealing.

I felt like I was on trial when I went down there. Linda wanted to know what I was made of. So when a nasty, brutish man refused to serve the girls a simple ice cream cone, I lit into him. These little girls, unmistakably Indian, had probably faced that kind of ignorance all their lives. Why, I'd put up with it all too often in my own life. I made up my mind that they'd never have to eat that particular meal of ugly stupidity while I was around.

We arranged to bring the girls home for a two-week Christmas vacation. A few days before the scheduled pickup I began to get cold feet. Our house was small; I wasn't really sure we had room for two. We didn't have much in the way of comfort to offer. I knew that two girls who'd spent virtually their whole lives in orphanages and foster homes would be tough customers. Linda had just about raised Jackie, and I didn't how she'd feel about my taking over the role of mother. Then too, Linda had a bad skin rash that made her face and body break out in running sores. Miss Joe told me they'd tried everything and still couldn't stop it from coming back time and again. It would always be with her. I knew that, and I guessed the girls might have other health problems too, as a result of their deprived upbringing. And finally—this was a big one—Was it fair to Gordon to bring two half-grown girls into his life?

I asked Pastor Cleamons about my dilemma. He advised me to look to the Bible for an answer. I think he knew there were passages I could find that would guide me in either direction, depending on what was truly in my heart. I followed his advice; for quite a while I couldn't find anything that really spoke to my doubts. Then I came across this message in Matthew; I believe it's Matthew 25:40: "What you do for one of the least of these, you do for me also." That was the reassurance I was looking for. If I followed my heart, we would be doing God's work. We really couldn't go wrong.

When we brought the girls home, I could see that Gordon was up in the air about the whole thing. He could be a little gruff when he was uncomfortable about something, and he was uncomfortable that first night. Jackie, who was a bold one, kind of won him over with her gumption. She grabbed onto his legs and said, "I want to stay here, Dad. I'm gonna stay here."

Linda was a much harder sell. I knew she was crazy about our black-and-white pinto, Cindy. But I didn't want to be accepted because of a horse. There had to something between us, and for a while that didn't seem to be in the cards. Then one night toward the end, while Linda was helping me wash the dishes, we made contact. Literally, in fact. The kitchen was tiny, and as we danced around the sink to wash and dry, we bumped hips. She gave me one of her looks and a shy smile. "Move over, Mama," she said. Just that. It was enough. I knew what it meant to call someone Mama. I'd done it for years.

The two weeks passed all too quickly. The girls didn't want to go back. "I wish I could break a leg so I'd get to stay here," Jackie gushed. Linda nodded her head in vigorous agreement. I wasn't any happier to drive them back than they were to be driven. We had a tearful parting, but I took them by the hands and told them that we really did love them, and I hoped to be back to get them for good. They didn't look like they believed me, but they did allow me to dry their eyes.

How I wanted those little girls. I started to think of them as my little Apache dolls, though of course I knew they were no such thing. Maybe I even hoped that they could take the place of the buried Delaware dolls; that they would restore balance in my world. Not that I was conscious of Grandma or the dolls or my own childhood right then, but down deeper that may have been my notion.

When I got home, I was surprised to see that Gordon had tears in his eyes. "What's wrong?" I asked. "Oh, nothing," he replied. He seemed a little embarrassed about his surrender to sentiment. I guess my eyes must have glistened with tears too, because he asked me what was wrong. I matched his reply. "Nothing," I said.

I didn't want to force Gordon into anything. I didn't want him to resent me later for his generosity today. "You want to keep them?" I asked. A world hung on his answer. He thought for a minute, nodded, and simply said, "Yes. How about you?" I didn't have to think any more about my answer; I'd gone over it in my mind a hundred times. "Oh yes, yes," I answered. And our world changed forever.

Sixteen

A NEW
BEGINNING

We didn't waste much time, Gordon and I, after we reached our decision. There was one more drive down to Muskogee. The girls brought few possessions back with them; one carton filled with Christmas gifts, and the clothes they wore. We wanted this to be a fresh start for the two of them, and that wasn't hard to arrange; the state brought them to us with almost nothing of their own.

Miss Joe did sit me down and talk to me at some length about Linda's skin problem. I was told that she would always break out, there was really nothing to do about it. I was given a list of foods that she could eat and that she shouldn't eat and detailed instructions for how to handle an attack of sores. I thought to myself that love would probably be the best medicine for those problems, so I had a talk with Linda and told her that we were starting fresh on everything. She would eat healthy food that I prepared for everyone, and we'd find out together what worked for her and what didn't. I told her that I thought she was a beautiful girl and that we would pray together for a healing. Well, I'm here to tell you that her skin got a whole lot better. I guess the doctors were right in the end, because the problem came back years later, but for the time I had her Linda wasn't really much troubled by skin sores. Back at Murrow the kids—the cruel ones, and there were plenty of them—had called her sore-faced Lakoe. Well she wasn't Lakoe anymore, and she sure wasn't sore-faced.

Speaking of names, they were definitely a part of the new start we had in mind for our little girls. I'd been a bestower of Delaware names since childhood, when Mama allowed me to do the honors for my younger brother and sisters. It gave me great pleasure to give my beautiful new daughters Indian names now; I felt that I was completing a circle. I thought Jackie looked just like a little bunny rabbit when she was at her cutest, so I named her Chëmamës. Once Linda drew that fabulous blue bird for me, she kind of chose her own name. I called her Okee-chee, Delaware for little bluebird. I wanted to give the girls names that told the world how sweet and special they were to me, and I thought those would do the trick. Certainly Linda has used hers throughout her life; it's become her professional name as an artist. Jackie enjoyed hers, I suppose, but she let it go as she grew up.

The adoption gave the girls a chance to make a more practical name change as well. When Gordon and I got ready to sign the adoption papers, we found that we could put down any names we wanted. So we gave the girls their choice—they could pick from the wide world of names any they thought suited them. Linda kept her first name but changed her middle name from Sherrill to Sharon. Later, when it turned out there were a half dozen Lindas in high school, she started to use Sharon more and more. Jackie came to us wearing the name Tevelee Sharon, but she had some definite ideas about names and changed them both.

The fresh start included a new wardrobe for each new daughter, which we had to accumulate slowly, finances being what they were. There was a new extended family for the girls to meet, and we arranged for get-togethers with the branches of the vast Perry clan and a trip down to Texas to meet the Reeves. I have to admit to a little disappointment in some of my people. I knew that here and there the girls would bump into prejudice in Oklahoma; I mean, I've lived my life here. But from my own families I didn't anticipate any such foolishness. It wasn't the adoption, either. Gordon's sister Dolores adopted Joyce just about the same time we brought Linda and Jackie into the family. Joyce, a pretty little white girl also halfway to grown, was embraced by the whole clan. My beautiful Indian daughters were . . . I'm not going to say they were snubbed or insulted, but the reception was cool, was distant. I felt it; they felt it. We all understood it; God knows, they'd already had to deal with more prejudice in their short lives than I ever did in mine. It put me in mind of Mama and her struggles; I even wrote her to ask what I could do to smooth the way for my babies. She wrote back and said I should love them, hold their hands, and wipe their noses; there was no way to change the world.

From one corner of the family the response was warmer. Gordon's brother Ray had a passel of boys. There were Gene and Danny and Carl and Johnny and Jack. Gordon and I took to having them out to our place—once we got a place—each summer. Gordon loved his girls, but I think he needed to have some boys around; boys who could fish, toss a hard ball, bale hay, work cattle. Now the boys took to our little girls, who were good runners and scrappers and could hold their own at basketball and catch. Linda could even put a worm on a hook, and Jackie would reluctantly clean the take of bass and crappie from our two ponds out back. She drew the line at catfish, with their slimy bodies and sharp fins; those the boys had to clean on their own. Ray's boys considered our girls kin, wholeheartedly and without reserve, from the very first.

Fresh starts weren't always possible. The girls carried hurts from hellish childhoods that I couldn't soothe with new names, new family, new adventures, even new love. Agitation would take hold of Linda and Jackie, then the dam would burst and a flood of painful memories would pour out. Calm followed for days or weeks, then the tension built again, followed by fresh revelations. I heard about beatings and long imprisonments in dark closets, about hunger and bone-chilling cold, about picking cotton until their little hands bled, about whiskey breath choking them and hard hands pawing, about foul words that left scars, belts that left scars, sticks and kicks that left scars. The words poured out, then, invariably, Jackie cried. Linda never cried, but she needed to be held and rocked and comforted every bit as much as her sister.

I'd had a wonderful growing-up, as you know; I understood what childhood could be and should be. These poor, precious girls had known none of that. I wanted to show them, while there was still time, what joy was, what freedom felt like. I wanted to pass on the gift; that's what being a parent is all about. Maybe I wanted to enjoy some of it again myself.

So we did things together, things that came out of my own fond memories. We'd go down to the little stream that runs through our property and pile up loose sticks to make a big bonfire. I'd bring down some wieners, a bag of marshmallows, and a pitcher of lemonade; we'd get ourselves some green sticks and have a roast. I know bonfires are supposed to be with friends, not with moms, but the country was pretty well fenced by now, and the kids didn't roam as free as they did in my day. Anyway, I loved bonfires when I was a kid, and I still got a kick out of them as a mom.

We'd sit by a big roaring fire, stuff ourselves, and swap stories. I'd tell the girls a lot of the things I've told you in this book; they'd tell me about school or whatever was going on in their lives. I especially liked to tell them about Grandma Wahoney.

I think they were a little bit skeptical about the part where she talked to the Otter People and the woodpecker dressed up like a little person, but they were fascinated by that too. I wanted my girls to know they were Indians and to be proud of their heritage; that's why I told them the stories from my own tribe. I guess to me Indian was Delaware, so I shared my heritage with them as much as I could. Maybe, looking back, I should have learned more about Apaches and passed that on to them. I don't know. Both of them, in their different ways, did connect to an Indian heritage as they grew up, maybe more than I ever did. The times had changed; people stopped running away from their cultures and turned back to embrace them. To some extent I did that myself. But that's tomorrow, and tomorrow never touched the long, lovely afternoons we spent eating and talking around a bonfire. When the flames burned down to embers, we'd carefully scrape the remains of our fire and feast into the creek so Gordon wouldn't know about our guilty pleasures. The little conspiracy seemed to draw us girls together.

The best hideaway of all was Bullet Ford on the Verdigris River. We've visited Bullet Ford before, that is to say, we've driven over the broad expanse of Oolagah Lake, whose waters now flood the ford, and paused to remember. Bullet Ford was about four miles from our place, the most perfect swimming hole I've ever known; and believe me, I've spent my share of time splashing in swimming holes on our eastern Oklahoma rivers and streams. Now, I'm not saying there might not be clearer, more invigorating spots on brooks bubbling out of the Colorado Rockies, but I'll take Bullet Ford and let you take your chances on finding a better. For one thing, we couldn't have had Bullet Ford more to ourselves if we'd owned title to the property. It was a couple of miles down a rutted dirt road, and then a bit of a hike on a foot path to the river's edge. Some of our veteran fishermen knew the spot; maybe it was Gordon or his fishing buddy Woody Hayes that turned us on to it, I don't remember. The point was that no one, swimmer or fisherman, ever troubled our tranquillity at Bullet Ford. We'd go with my great friend Shug Hayes whenever we could. I'd load up our old green Chevy with picnic basket, towels, and kids and drive on to the Hayes place. Or Shug would fetch us in her somewhat newer model. Shug had two kids of her own, a boy and a girl, just a little younger than my two, and they loved to swim and splash at Bullet Ford every bit as much as Linda and Jackie. Shug's husband, Woody, worked with explosives; Gordon worked with fire in the oil tanks. The holders of the two most dangerous jobs in our country were natural buddies; together they were murder on the big river cats that grew to fifty pounds or more in our slow, muddy waters. Shug and I had our own things in common; we were moms of like-aged children and pillars of the church. We both loved the country and knew the ripening times of its fruits and flowers. We knew the joys of hard work and sweet leisure. We brought the stews and casseroles that people gobbled up at the church potlucks. Shug had some Cherokee to match up with my Delaware; I could share Indian memories with her. She was one who supported the adoption wholeheartedly and not falseheartedly. Bullet Ford was a place for memories, an Indian place. It should have been called Flint Ford; the sheer number of scrapers, knives, arrowheads, and axes was far greater than the few lumps of lead from a later time. After a rain, the steep little dirt track running down to the river would wash away, leaving flints pocking the roadside like lizard skin. All you had to do was pry them out, clean off the clay, and . . . well, some would have done a museum proud. We kept only the best. Most often Shug and I could sun and gossip on the rocks while the kids industriously scrambled up and back and up again, laying their treasure before us. They got to be pretty good at separating out the really fine pieces. Linda and Jackie both could tell the scrapers from the spears from the arrowheads. That wasn't really what counted; the thing I especially liked about it was that those arrowheads got us wondering about the people who made them. Shug and I would tell the kids what we'd heard and remembered about the Cherokee and Delaware settlements back in the far-off time, before statehood. But we didn't know why there were so many arrowheads here at Bullet Ford. The kids had lots of suggestions, and mostly they involved Indians ambushing white folks—soldiers or civilians, didn't matter. They'd get all wide-eyed and high-strung and laugh about some sort of massacre, and Shug and I would laugh along with them. I don't really know why.

The Verdigris got wide and mostly shallow at Bullet Ford. Shug and I would search out the holes and sudden deeps each time, because they changed position, and we'd make sure the kids knew just where they were. Then we could pretty much leave them to their own devices. The water flowed cool and swift and seemed cleaner than the rest of the river, like the little suspended particles of dirt and leaf that gave the Verdigris its name couldn't keep up with the joyful rush of water over flat rock. On the hottest days, we'd all lie on the flats and let the river massage the heat and weariness out of our bodies. Those were sweet, sweet times. Lying in the shallows, I'd think of Grandma Wahoney and her adventure with the Otter People. Sometimes I'd imagine that I caught a glimpse of an otter, the ripples of a diving otter, just beyond clear sight. Maybe I did. I might even pretend that I saw Grandma herself, up on the bank gathering herbs. I know, of course, that I didn't. But it is true that Grandma lived much of her life along rivers, as Delawares have since time past remembering. I felt so very comfortable, alone with the kids and my great friend, in the seclusion of our hideaway. I doubt whether Grandma

Wahoney, pushed to move again and again, ever felt as at home in her country as I felt in mine. The Delaware people—like so many tribes—were tied to our homeland by strands of memory and myth, of ceremony and spirit. We called the earth we loved our mother. Her dust creased our skin; it lined our lungs and swam in our blood. That's the way I feel about my homeland. As I sunned and swam at Bullet Ford, I wondered whether, in three centuries and more, our wandering tribe had felt the same communion with a place as I did with the land I so dearly loved.

Come evening, when the heat broke, we might pile up a bonfire from all the brush and driftwood on the bank and roast and sing. I'll tell you, I still think about the times we had at Bullet Ford. When they built the dam and flooded out the ford, I mourned its loss like I've mourned the loss of so many things I've loved. But that came later; now, when the girls were growing up, it was the secret and special place where we had our best times.

School was part of the fresh start for Linda and Jackie. They'd told me some stories about that school in Muskogee where the town kids ganged up and threw rocks at them. I knew things would be better at the Waller School, our two-room stone schoolhouse that was so much like the one I went to when I was a girl. I didn't have any illusions about country schools; I'm no romantic, and I lived through them. But I was pretty sure they'd be easier to keep an eye on than in the big city schools with their confusion of classrooms and bathrooms. I expected that some of the kids would be ignorant and mean, that they'd tease and taunt. There were other Indian kids at Waller; but they were Indians like me, pale and quiet about it. Linda and Jackie were near enough to full-bloods, and their kinship to Geronimo and his ilk could hardly be denied. So I knew there'd be some nonsense they'd have to put up with, and I wanted to make sure it never got out of hand.

My solution was that I came to be the cook for the forty or so students at Waller School. Now, I'd never cooked professionally for a crowd, but my experience flipping flapjacks for all those hungry Reeves back at the home place must have stood me in good stead, because I had no trouble with it. I'd drive the girls the mile or so to school and fire up the big gas stove. Ten, fifteen kids each day would come to school with empty bellies, and I'd fix a mess of pancakes or grits and eggs or omelets with ham and cheese. I think that as the year went on, more and more of the children would come to school without eating breakfast. I took that as a great compliment to my cooking. I'd bake up loaves of bread every day, fresh and hot. We got varieties of meat and great sacks of beans, potatoes, and rice from some level of government, and our local farm families would supplement the larder with beans and carrots and turnips and canned goods of one kind or another. I'd fry up some burgers or prepare a big pot of beans and ham or beef stew. There was a doorway with no door between my kitchen and the classrooms, and sometimes the aroma of baking bread and bubbling stew filled the crowded stone rooms and the nostrils and bellies of the restless children. Big eyes stared at the doorway, trying to divine the secrets of the noon meal. It got so the teachers—who were very good, we were lucky in them—didn't schedule anything demanding for the half hour before noon. They would tease me that my lunch was taking over the school day, but they dived in to the food with the same enthusiasm as most of the kids.

My work as cook served several purposes. I got to keep an eye on my girls. I didn't really see much in the way of problems. The grade-school kids were better about these things than their elders—Indian, white, it didn't seem to matter. Linda was a good little athlete; she was on the school basketball team along with another Indian girl and three whites. We were a tiny school, and the team didn't win a whole lot—breaking even was considered quite a triumph. But there are things that count more than victory, more important lessons to learn, and they learned them. It wasn't until later, till high school, that race prejudice—Oklahoma's curse and America's—showed itself in many slights and discriminations. And I couldn't be there to watch, to step in. I suppose that's the way of things in the wide world. But our little community of Winganon, our tiny fortress Waller School, offered the girls a four-year easement from the prejudice that has dogged them, one way or another, much of their life. I'm kind of proud of that.

One of the joys we could offer our girls in their new lives was the company of pets. There are two kind of pets on the farm—the ones you choose and the ones that choose you. Let me tell you a little about that second kind, which urban folks likely don't know anything about. On the farm, we have animals with a primary purpose—hens that lay eggs, for instance, cows that give milk and produce the beef cattle that are our principal cash crop. They're not there for our amusement or company, but sometimes they surprise us by revealing a personality. It isn't necessarily a pleasant personality. We had Beauregard the rooster and Holly the goose, who defined foul and fair in the world of fowl. Beauregard performed all the tasks a rooster does on a farm: waking us religiously at 5 A.M., rain or shine, keeping the hens happily laying, maintaining a certain order in the barnyard. He was also a vicious brute who pecked at legs and attacked us, wings flapping and spurs flying. I know he made egg gathering tough for the girls. For the first few years—before we brought running water and a toilet into the house—we'd all have to take a stick along to beat off Beauregard on our trips to the outhouse. I guess nowadays the experts would say he was territorial. We had another name for it. By contrast, our big gray-and-white goose

Holly was such a sweetie that she quickly moved herself off our menu and became our pet. I'd know when the girls were coming up the walk from high school because Holly would fly down to greet them, squawking in excitement. She'd alight behind them, her wings spread, her big neck craned, and usher them home, lumbering along on her stubby legs. I'd see Holly combing the girls' hair with her bill, very gently as it seemed. You tend to get seeds and such snarling your hair—it's a hazard of country living. The girls would shout their complaints when I tried to run a comb through the tangles; they seemed to prefer Holly's efforts. Holly quickly showed a talent as a sort of guard goose, trumpeting and honking at every stranger's approach. When she spread her wings and fluffed out the feathers on her head, she could present a formidable appearance. Her violent hiss had the same effect as running a nail over a chalkboard; it was an intimidating sound. Holly helped me run off a couple of hunters when Gordon was away. She won us over to thinking of her as a pet; eventually it was Beauregard, after one too many attacks on company, who ended up in the soup pot.

Holly had plenty of help when it came to protecting the home place. Our dog Buster—the girls called him Buster the Wonder Dog—was maybe forty pounds of black-and-brown all-American, but his heart must have weighed eighty pounds. Like many farm dogs, Buster had various roles to play. Cowherd, protector, snake hunter, hero. He was nimble; he was fearless; he was boundlessly energetic and fiercely loyal. The girls loved him; they showered him with affection and sneaked table scraps to him behind my back.

They had their reasons. For one thing, our quick little dog was death on snakes. We have snakes, killer snakes, both with rattles and silent. You never know when a copperhead is lurking in the tall grass or a moccasin is going to swim by the calm shallows at Bullet Ford. The rattlers did give you a little warning, but it generally didn't help much. Buster didn't need warning; somehow he knew, and he struck before they could. There was the time Jackie reached into the grain bin, pulled out an armload of corn and copperhead, and barely got the scream out of her mouth before Buster had ripped the snake out of her arms. Buster came along on our Bullet Ford picnics. He would sit on shore and stare at the water, watching out for snakes. Many's the time his bark would alert us to a "stick" writhing in the water; we'd call the kids out until it disappeared. Buster was helpful to me when we had to deal with the human snakes who trespass on farms with their liquor and guns and shoot at whatever their fogged imaginations suppose is a deer. Once the kids came to live with us, our tolerance for that sort of dangerous foolishness just dried up. Buster would set up a terrific yapping when he caught wind of them, and Gordon ran them right off. Sometimes it fell to me to get rid of the trespassers; I was grateful to have Buster by my side. He had a way of bristling and growling and looking about twice his normal size. I'm remembering a couple of times when Buster played a big part in persuading some drunks with guns to take their leave of our place. So, yes, I'll go along with the girls in calling Buster our wonder dog.

If Buster was our wonder dog, then Cindy was surely our wonder horse. Cindy was my mount before the girls came to live with us. They quickly claimed my pony; or I should say that Linda did. I saw right away how enthralled Linda was with my beautiful black-and-white pinto. I bowed to a passion that was so strong it bewildered me. I officially gave the horse to both girls a few months after they arrived. Linda took to riding right away and soon became an expert young horsewoman. Jackie was afraid of Cindy and a clumsy rider to boot; after a few attempts she gave up on riding altogether. For Linda's next birthday, Jackie drew a picture of a horse's rear end, which I guess she assumed was her half, and wrote "She's all yours, Sis" on the card. From that day forward there was no dispute about who owned Cindy.

Linda had all the care of her pony. She fed Cindy, watered her, groomed her, threw the heavy saddle on her back, and placed the bit in her mouth. Linda did most of her riding right on our place; it had hills and streams and fences to jump. When she saddled Cindy up, I'd warn her not to gallop or jump fences, and she'd solemnly agree. But I knew that she raced the wind and jumped whatever was in her way just as soon as she got out of sight. After all, I'd had a horse and parents myself once.

Speaking of parents, Gordon and I were certainly a part of the fresh start our girls had to deal with and, for Linda at least, maybe the most unpalatable part. Jackie had no trouble with it; she was younger, for one thing. She'd always been the child; I'm not sure that my regime was any stricter than Linda's. In fact, acting the baby was a big part of Jackie's charm. For Linda it was altogether different. Linda had been mother and father both to little Jackie — seeing that her sister got her fair share of food, even when it meant Linda had to do without, fighting Jackie's battles, keeping the little girl in line so there weren't so many battles to fight. I know it was hard for her to give up being a parent, but I thought that if we were ever going to be a real family, she'd have to do it. Then, too, Linda simply isn't inclined to do what other people tell her. Not under any circumstances. I suppose that's part of the same heritage from child care — the stubbornness, the pride. Linda had a hard time believing anyone really loved her; the trust just wasn't there.

So, to say it straight, we had some battles. She challenged me with many little defiances; I didn't think I could let them pass. One that stands out was the battle of the broom. I remember it this way; she may have a different recollection. I asked her to sweep the kitchen; she left a sizable pile of dirt in the middle of the floor. I asked again; the dirt remained. I suggested she do it right; the dirt was still there. Neither of us raised our voice, but we went round and round in the same way maybe a dozen times, for what seemed like hours. Finally she did sweep all the dirt off that kitchen floor. That was probably our Gettysburg, though I don't suppose it was anything extraordinary in the annals of mother-daughter confrontations. There were all sorts of lesser struggles—meals eaten cold, chores done after dark. I had no experience in mothering orphan children, and I thought that certain patterns of long standing had to be broken. Maybe I was harsh; I don't know. I don't think you can ever know. I'm sure the impression I'm creating here is exaggerated; we had more sunny days at the swimming hole than confrontations in the kitchen.

I did take special pains with the girls' Christian education. They'd both been baptized years before, and they'd spent their share of Sundays in church, but I didn't think their acquaintance with the Bible was up to standard. One thing you could say about most of our Winganon children was that they knew the book. In fact, our Winganon Baptist Church ran a Bible camp over on Flynt Creek that had good food and some very nice activities. The way you qualified for a two-week camp session was to memorize and recite Bible verses. It was important to me that the girls distinguish themselves in this exercise. I'd help them with the memory work, grilling and correcting until they had the verses down pat. Then we'd go over to recite before Mr. Heck, who kept track of all the church children's progress. Not only did Jackie and Linda master the three hundred verses they needed to win a free camp session every year they were eligible, they were near the top of the list each year. I felt then, and continue to believe, that a good knowledge of the Bible is a vital part of any child's upbringing. I think that it was a valuable corrective to some of the terrible things the girls had been exposed to during all those years of abuse. And, I'll admit it, I wanted to let the few high and mighty among us know that my little Apache girls, who'd grown up without benefit of family and with little knowledge of the book, could hold their own with the children of Winganon. I guess you could say that in this instance I was feeling Indian and proud. Linda and Jackie never let me down, and I've always been grateful to them for that.

The years when my girls went to grade school and church, rode horseback, frolicked at Bullet Ford, came on cookouts, helped me and, yes, defied me, memorized their verses and did me proud, were a kind of return to paradise—as close as I've ever come to that. In one sense it was even better. You see, Jesus had come into my life, and that changes everything. This good time wasn't something I was born into. With the help of our Lord, it was something I worked hard to make happen. When I think about it that way, I feel pretty good about myself.

Seventeen

THE FAMILY OF
MY OLD AGE

When you look at life in a certain light, it's all about family. And I don't mean what we've come to call the nuclear family. My Delaware people understood that we're related, in a sense, to all the people we care about—the people who care about us. I think that's especially true as we get older and one cast of characters fades from our life. If we're lucky, they're replaced by others. I've been lucky.

You've visited the family of my youth and the family of my adult years. Now it's time to walk with me on that fond, familiar road until we see its end—the far horizon.

My girls gave me love and comfort for a time. But they had their own destinies to discover, their own work to do, their own families to raise. Inevitably, things changed. Linda's energy and enthusiasm gave Cindy, already an old horse, a new lease on life, but by the time the girls were ready for high school, Cindy faltered. Time marches on, whether we will or no, and before you know it your children are in their teens. It happens too quickly, even when you have the full eighteen or so years; Gordon and I had half that time.

The teen years were not my best time, and frankly the prospect of teenage daughters worried me more than a little. Linda and Jackie didn't have to live through the depression, but the sixties, in their own way, were a tough time for parents and children. I wasn't prepared for the brave new world that was dawning; I don't suppose many parents were. To give you an idea — this was the first lightning bolt in what I thought was a clear sky — there was the Elvis appearance on the Ed Sullivan show. We'd all settled down to watch; Gordon really liked the Sullivan show. I had no idea that anything out of the ordinary was scheduled. Even when they announced Elvis Presley I didn't react; I'd never heard of him, to tell you the truth. I saw a stirring, an excitement in my girls, though. A few minutes later the young people in the crowd — and there were lots of them — commenced to screaming. This good-looking, oily young man came on the TV and started to sing in a way that was unlike anything I'd ever heard before. The camera panned the audience; girls were shrieking and fainting. Linda and Jackie were wide-eyed with excitement. When the camera returned to that young man, he was swiveling and flipping his hips in the most suggestive way. I'll admit it; I was one of the mothers who stood up and physically blocked the TV screen on that momentous night.

It seemed as though I spent the next few years blocking TV screens, so to speak. There was a generation gap in the Perry home, not bitter and hateful, but undeniable and bewildering. I had hoped that at least one of the girls might become a Baptist missionary — that had always seemed to me an especially useful and exciting way of life — but it became clear that such a future simply was not to be. The girls had their own stars to follow, and right after graduating from high school they began to do just that.

Jackie married — a man I could not welcome or respect. Linda went off to the new Institute of American Indian Arts in Santa Fe, looking to discover herself. I'd always believed she could be an artist and tried to encourage her in my way, but I was surprised at the direction she chose. Linda studied drama and dance. Now, Baptists just aren't comfortable with either drama or dance; we consider them sensual and dangerous. I felt like she was rejecting our values, trying so hard to run away from rural Oklahoma that she wasn't careful about what she was running to. We tried to be supportive from a distance, but I just couldn't embrace what my daughters were doing with their lives. It would be fair to say that we grew apart in those years.

First Jackie and then Linda made her way to Chicago, where they began to make lives for themselves. Now, I've been to Chicago quite a number of times, visiting them, and I've never really felt comfortable there. It has a reputation in my part of the country, Chicago does, as a sinful town, a gangster town. Nothing I've seen there suggests to me that the reputation is undeserved.

In 1975 Linda married Manny Skolnick, which led, among other things, to this book. The wedding, as I understand, was a modest one. Gordon and I didn't go; we were pretty much estranged from the girls at that time. Linda and Manny did visit us on their honeymoon. I'll admit it, we were a little nervous about that visit. Manny was a Chicagoan born and bred, and that didn't seem to bode well. Also, we had little experience with Jewish people in our part of the world, so that was another question in our minds. He was kind of wild looking when he burst out of the car—hair very long and curly. The word hippie came to mind; I'd heard about them, but he was the first one who ever hugged me. Yes, he did hug me and shook hands vigorously with Gordon. He seemed comfortable on the farm; I think over the years our place has been a kind of country home for him.

It came to me on that first meeting that this was going to be all right. And that's how it's turned out. Things have been good between Linda's family and me. I got to watch my four grandchildren grow up. They drove out to visit us once or twice a year, and after Gordon passed I flew in to Chicago just enough to be able to tolerate the place. Linda's two oldest children, Tevelee and Quentin, came out on their own to spend time with us, and we shared some adventures. Now I'm looking forward to getting to know their babies, my great-grandchildren. With the younger two, Naomi and Vonda, I was already a bit too old to take them on my own when they reached the age where they could travel. But they come along often with their folks, and I've watched them grow into beautiful young ladies.

Although I often find myself wishing they were closer, I've come to believe it's a good thing Linda moved to a city like Chicago. I think she needed a bigger stage to play out her life on than anything we could provide here in Winganon. She keeps me posted, and I must tell you how proud I am of her many involvements, her real accomplishments. She's always busy, always on the go, on boards of directors, organizing art events, judging shows, lecturing, hosting events at the art gallery she owned for ten years. Sometimes she'll send me a press clipping about something she's involved with, and I'll show it around to my friends at church. I keep all of Winganon up to date on Linda's activities; sometimes people ask me how she does it all, and I have to say that I don't really know. Good upbringing, I guess. And I smile. Through it all, she's managed to raise up her four lovely children. I have to tell you I'm impressed. I don't know if I've ever told her that, but I'll do it here and now. Sharon, honey (she's been calling herself Sharon for years, so I'll do it here), you've done me proud.

When Linda and Manny came out to see us, and we made our peace, Jackie followed suit. At that time Jackie was still the little sister, and she kind of tagged along in many things. We've kept in touch through good times and bad. Life hasn't been easy for Jackie and her three daughters. Sometimes I've shaken my head in sorrow and wonderment; sometimes I've applauded their efforts and shared laughter; always I've tried to lend a hand. Of course, you want things to be better for your children, your friends, the ones you love—better than life sometimes allows things to be. I doubt if there's anyone alive who hasn't felt that from time to time. Linda and Jackie both had some terrible things to contend with from a very young age. One was made strong by her struggle, the other, I guess, was wounded by hers. For one I could wish more courage and honor, for the other more faith. They could probably wish something for me. For all that, we're mother and daughters still.

One thing I'm proud of in both my daughters is the strength of their Indian ties. Linda has been a pillar of Chicago's Indian world for a long time, planning and staging events, championing art and artists, exhibiting at powwows. Jackie too is very comfortable in the Indian world of potlucks and powwows; many of her friends are, as she would say, skins. I think it's great that women today can be openly, aggressively, and proudly Indian. That was pretty hard for me to do in Oklahoma forty or fifty years ago.

Inevitably, especially as we grow old, life becomes a long series of good-byes. Of course I've had my share of good-byes, some of them terribly hard; at eighty-two, most of the people you've lived your life with have preceded you to the grave. But I've also been very lucky. I've had many hellos in my life; even late in life. It seems that I've been able to live always supported by loving hands, rocked in the arms of church and family. Thanks to that support, I've stayed on, proud and independent, at the one spot I love best in the world. I want to tell you about the good-byes and hellos in my life, and to nod in deep appreciation to the new family that has supported and sustained me in what, to this hour, has been a serene and pleasant old age.

Let me begin with the good-byes. Not all, just the three that shocked me at the core of my being. Mama. Gordon. Ruth.

Papa died down in Texas, and Mama, who always preferred Oklahoma, moved back up here. Her health wasn't good; she had some surgeries, and Linda had to nurse her for a time. Then something remarkable happened; at seventy-five Mama found herself a man, an old cowboy who had a kind heart and a good sense of fun. They got married, and she had some good years with him. Although I'm not inclined to follow her example, I admire it and am grateful to this day that she found happiness at the end. I'm not sure all her daughters agreed, be that as it may, but I am confident that Papa would have given his approval. That thought tempered my sadness when she died, at what then seemed the ripe age of seventy-eight. But it was hard to say good-bye to the woman who had been our strength for all the years of my life.

When Gordon passed, it was so sudden it jolted me. True, he'd known pain, maybe every day of his life for forty years, his back was that bad. But he was lean and straight and strong and looked to me much less than his seventy years. I fully expected that he would outlive me and worried sometimes about how he would get his food cooked just so and who would provide him with all the small comforts he'd come to expect from me. Then, on a sunny morning in early fall, 1984, Gordon complained of a pain in his shoulder. An hour later he fell to the ground. I could see right away that it was bad. I didn't know CPR; I tried to hold and comfort him, but by the time the ambulance got to our place he was gone. Linda and Manny and the two older kids drove out the next day; I let my family and neighbors do what needed to be done.

The church community rallied round, supplying a tremendous feast for the wake and all the love and support they thought I could handle. I'm not sure I responded the way I should have. The world had shifted under my feet; I was standing on quicksand. Soon enough the crowd left, family returned home, and I was left alone with my grief and bewilderment. It seemed that I bumped into ghosts at every turn; my cozy little house was haunted by memories of Gordon. I'd see him in shadows, or smell him just around the corner. I didn't think I could escape the press of memory while I lived in my dear, familiar house. The night, especially, held terrors, and I had never before given the dark a second thought. Our isolation, which had always been a comfort, became a threat. The country night is full of sound, and I heard the footsteps of vandals in every flutter of wings or scurry of possum or skunk. It got so I shuttered the windows, loaded my shotguns and spread them through the house, and slept with a loaded gun when I slept at all.

Linda must have heard the strain in my voice. She called around to some of my friends and, before I knew it, flew down here to straighten her old mother out. I was never so happy to see anyone; I really needed the company. It took some nerve for her to stay with me; with all the guns around, I'm afraid she thought I might hear her going to the toilet and shoot. Linda helped me find some answers. We arranged for the big light in my yard that makes it almost impossible for anyone to sneak up in the dark. We unloaded the guns and packed them away. I opened myself up to the neighbors and friends who wanted to help but were put off by what they saw as my standoffishness. I began to live my life again.

My sister Ruth died just a year ago, after a series of strokes and a gradual collapse. Her two children and two sisters were with her through the long ordeal. I stayed down in Beaumont for more than a month, and the bedside vigil became a wearying ordeal for all of us. I felt that I had to get back for a bit to put my own affairs in order, but I was feeling weary for such a long drive. So Linda and Manny drove down to Beaumont, said good-bye to Ruth, and helped me get back to my farm. Linda accompanied me in my car; she doesn't drive, but she did keep my eyes open and my mind focused. She may live far away, but she's close enough when it really counts.

The good-byes have been hard. But I've been lucky enough to have had my share of hellos, even late in life. I've never felt isolated or lonely; there have always been people I cared for who cared for me. I've always known that hands would reach out to steady me, to support me, to comfort me, when I needed those things. I've been able to savor the pleasures of my solitude because I knew it was never absolute. It was my choice to spend what time I did alone, dreaming on my porch, watching cottontails play hopscotch on my lawn and scissortails follow the leader on the electric wires.

Many of the dear friends of my later years have come from our church. Shug Hayes, dear Shug, as it turned out, has been there for me long after Bullet Ford disappeared under the waves. Then there's Katherine Johns, who lives just up the road. Sometimes she comes on down when the clouds are green and the air's heavy; I have a storm cellar and she doesn't. We'll sit in the cozy shadowland and talk about old times while the hail rattles against my heavy tin door. But even when there's hardly a cloud in the sky, she'll drop in and suggest an adventure. We both appreciate a good meal and enjoy food more with good company. I think she's good company; she thinks the same of me.

Some of my family of age are literal family, one member stepping in when another departs. I must introduce you to the ones who have been family in every sense of the word.

A great companion of my old age was Gordon's big sister, Maisel Shipley, who could do some things her brother couldn't. Maisel, trim, straight, and strong, who kept a perfectly ordered house in Bartlesville, who bowled in a league until her ninetieth birthday. Maisel, who shows Bartlesville a formal face but who loves to travel and knows how to kick up her heels. Maisel, who helped me explore the world as Gordon never could. We took a wonderful trip to Spain and North Africa. We went to London, Paris, Germany, and beyond on a trip where I got sick and, I'm afraid, cramped her style. We enjoyed sun and surf together on the Alabama Gulf Coast. We shared what has surely been the most thrilling day of my life. From Gibraltar, we crossed over into Morocco. We ate lunch in a restaurant up on a cliff, looking down on mud houses pressed against the rock wall. They looked like the little hives of mud dauber wasps on my porch back home; we were that high up. As we ate spicy, wonderful dishes, they filled the stage with exotic African types for us American tourists—a snake charmer, a giant black man beating a tambourine and glistening in the sun, a belly dancer doing things I'd never seen before. We went shopping in a bazaar, so busy and noisy, where I bought a wonderful rug that I still treasure. We actually rode on a camel; boy, you're high off the ground on the back of a camel. Finally, as we were heading back to the boat, Maisel bought a big old basket from a man running alongside our buggy, for us to carry the rug in. What a day that was. Sometimes Maisel and I get together for lunch over in Bartlesville and just shake our heads and laugh about some of the times we've had.

When Ruth got old and infirm her children, Lita and Robert, stepped into the breach. I've enjoyed Beaumont more in their company than ever before. In fact, Lita and I have made that trip down to Texas our shared adventure.

With Lita, I suppose travel was in the stars. Ruth birthed Lita at the Indian hospital near Bartlesville. When she felt the baby coming, we had to find a way to get to the hospital. Ruth and I set out walking to where we knew her husband's grandfather, Grandpa

Vincent, was selling buttermilk and such from his horse-drawn cart. When we caught up with him, Grandpa Vincent drove us over to the hospital. I don't think that old cart ever went quicker.

Now, fast-forward sixty years or so. Gordon is gone, my kids have moved away. Ruth and Indie are down in Texas, not much inclined or really able to visit me. Comes an occasion, Thanksgiving or Christmas or a birthday, Lita and I drive the four hundred miles or so down to Beaumont together. We do it many times; it gets to feel like the route down U.S. 69 and 75 is our own private roadway. We know where to pick up the sweetest peaches in season, where to get a great breakfast on the road. We share the driving, share the talk and adventure of a long haul in the car.

Lita is companion; her brother Robert is a big part of the destination. Kind, generous, open-hearted and -minded, Robert lived with his mother and nursed her through her worst times, as she nursed him. He's always good company and a good host; since Ruth passed on, he's made Lita and me feel welcome in his house.

I truly am blessed. Whenever someone moves on or passes on, it seems someone else takes their place. Carl Perry and his dear wife Peggy along with their sweet little girls, Ashley and Carmen, have stepped in to replace my girls and the grandchildren who've become adults.

I couldn't live on my own, out in the country, without all the love and help Carl and Peggy have given me. Peggy's the most energetic and good-hearted girl. She helps me clean up my house, keeps my yard mowed, does some of my shopping, looks in on me at all hours. In addition to caring for two little girls, I guess you could say she cares for me. On top of that, she's so important to our church—on all the planning committees, bringing big pots of good hot food to our picnics. Carl works hard at the airport over in Tulsa, which means a lot of driving every day. He's a clever man who fixes up little gizmos that make it easier for me to do things that have suddenly become hard. These are things I never used to even think about, like turning my ignition key or stepping over my stoop without stumbling.

I've had the pleasure of watching their two girls grow up from babies. They both call me Aunt Nette, climb up on my lap and give me hugs. Just like my real grandkids used to do when they were visiting years ago. It's such a pleasure to have that kind of loving on hand every day.

There's another reason I rely so much on Carl and Peggy, and I'm afraid I have to mention it. You see, I've developed an allergic reaction to food that closes up my throat and sets my heart racing. What's puzzling is that it's so unpredictable; you just can't tell what's going to trigger it. Many's the time Peggy's had to bundle up her babies, give me a shot of antihistamine, and rush me over to the Indian hospital. It's a scary time for all of us, and I'm just so grateful she's been here to do it.

In my world, among the family and friends who've eased my way into my eighties, I am allowed to believe that age is a valuable thing. I am treated like someone who has acquired a measure of wisdom, just as old people were treated for years and centuries but are too seldom treated today.

I've found that the last years, like the first, can be a joy if they are lived well. The pleasures of age are much different from the pleasures of youth, but they are every bit as satisfying.

Eighteen

THE DELAWARE
PATH

There are many, many things that family brings to a happy life—love, understanding, help when you need it, good company. But there are some things no one else can do for you, that you have to do for yourself

No one can heal your deepest hurts for you. No one else can make you whole. No one, that is, but Jesus. I guess what I'm saying is that salvation is from God, and each of us has to find the acceptance of it in our own heart. Christ can show the way; the church can help. Sometimes help can come from other places, surprising sources. I got help from Grandma Wahoney.

After the girls moved out of the house and Gordon and I were left once again to our own devices, I started to look into my Delaware heritage. One of our local women took to writing native genealogies. I met her, talked with her, bought her book. I didn't really like what it said about Grandma and the Delaware dolls, so I decided to see what I could find out on my own. I thought there were answers in my own head, forgotten episodes from my childhood, memories buried just like Grandma's dolls had been buried. I had to find a way to get at them.

I went to some powwows with my cousin Leona, who'd gone to the stomp dances and such with us sixty years before. Leona had beautiful old Delaware clothes; she looked just wonderful when she dressed in all her finery. It felt good to go back. But I had no costume of my own; I didn't feel a part of it. I remained an outsider in my own mind.

I started to do some reading; I had to learn the history and lore of my own people from books. Not just from books; often it seemed that something I read in a book would trigger a memory. The story I told you about Mama eating for Rosie Longbone, that was something I'd forgotten until the reading brought it back to mind.

At about the same time, a project came up that pushed me closer to the Delaware dolls. I found that the old Beck cemetery, the Delaware cemetery where many of my relatives were buried, had gone to ruin. I went out to see for myself and found tombstones tipped over, fence vandalized, a tangle of brush and brambles, some graves that looked like they were about to slide into the Caney River with the next flood.

The ruin shocked me. This might have been the resting place of Grandma Wahoney, the matriarch of my line, the ground she'd trusted to embrace her Delaware dolls for eternity. And now it was a weed patch that could become a true horror should the river flood. For some reason, it was the dolls that troubled me. Grandma's spirit was in heaven, I knew that. But the dolls . . . Who knew about the dolls? There must have been something of the spirit attached to them, but I didn't really understand it. I dreamed about the dolls; they called out to me from their dark resting place. They wanted something from me; I didn't know what it was.

I did what I could to help restore Beck cemetery. I was too old to cut brush, but I donated what money we could afford to help get the job done. I'd go out and check on the progress from time to time, and it was heartwarming. They did a good job, I'll tell you that. They cleared the brush, rebuilt the fence, moved the threatened gravesites. Now the old Beck cemetery truly is hallowed ground for our elders, a fitting resting place for Grandma and her dolls.

According to the Delaware way of thinking, I was feeding myself, feeding my spirit, with these new interests. I found myself wondering about Grandma Wahoney, as I hadn't in years. Of course I'd told the girls the Grandma stories, but that wasn't much different from the Three Bears or the legends of King Arthur. Now I studied her photo, searching out the secret of her strength. What could it have been like to be 108 years old, wise in a language and lifeway that scarcely anyone knew, perfectly suited to a way of life that had ceased to be? I wanted to know Grandma's face better than I could just by looking at her photos. Maybe my own aging had something to do with my new interest; Grandma at over a century made me feel young.

The dolls in the cemetery, Grandma's photos . . . they started to come together for me. I knew that I couldn't literally exhume the dolls; they would have become unrecognizable by now. I knew something about dollmaking. I'd made dolls exuberantly as a child, timidly as an adult, using a premade foundation. I toyed with the idea of making replicas of the Delaware dolls, but I rejected that. I didn't know enough about what they really looked like, for one thing. Besides, the idea seemed like sacrilege; the dolls were spiritual objects that I had no right to take for my own. I wasn't close enough to the world they came from; I don't think anyone is today.

The idea came to me; I would make a Grandma Wahoney doll. A doll in the likeness of the Doll Keeper: the idea intrigued and excited me. I wanted to build it from scratch—head, hands, shoes, pipe, body, clothes, all. I wasn't sure what material to use. Not mud from the riverbank; not for this. I wanted something that would take fine detail, that I could fire in my home. I searched the craft shops and discovered a compound that molds easily and bakes hard in the oven. Now I was ready.

It's a funny thing, but I didn't have to look at Grandma's photos when I worked on her. Her face was that clear in my mind. Which is not to say the work came easy. It must have been weeks that I went over her wizened features to get them exactly the way I wanted. Grandma had thin, fine lips, just a line, really, yet in her photos the lower lip protruded. It was an expression of defiance, just the look I wanted on the doll. And the wrinkles, fine like parchment; I had to get those right. She wore gold hoop earrings; I used little links from a bracelet and put them right in the compound. Finally I thought the likeness was perfect and I put the clay head, hollowed at the neck, in the oven. I held my breath while that head baked; I'd spent so much time, and I wasn't sure how it would come out. But it was perfect. Then I modeled her hands — gnarled, strong, with the stubby little pipe she always carried in her right hand. She wore boots; I made those. I put holes in the hands and boots so I could attach them to the body. When everything was fired, I painted it with acrylic paint. That was a pretty delicate operation too, I'll tell you.

I planned on Grandma being about eight inches tall; that's how big I made the clay parts. Next I built what I like to call a skeleton from pipe cleaners — body, arms, legs, neck — and tied and glued on the head, hands, and feet. I wrapped stuffing around the pipe cleaners, tying it on with string. Then I sewed pieces of Gordon's socks around the stuffing. It looked like underwear, which was suitable, since Grandma wore leather leggings in all seasons.

I didn't have any doubts about what Grandma would wear. You see, years and years ago Mama kept a dress of Grandma's. I hadn't seen it since I was about ten, but I remembered everything about it. It was blue, a blue floral print dress in the style of the late nineteenth century. It had a long skirt, full sleeves, a high lace collar. Beneath the skirt, a full petticoat. I could close my eyes and see that dress, lonely on its form, in a corner of our second floor.

One thing I found as I made the doll was that I remembered a great deal about Grandma Wahoney, more than I'd supposed. I never met the old woman; she was five years in her grave when I was born. And yet she lived in my mind with a vividness that attached to few of the people I'd actually known as a child. I can't explain it; I accept it as a blessing.

I felt tremendous satisfaction, bordering on relief, when I finished the doll. I was proud of her, proud of myself for being able to make her. Nothing else that I've ever made provided the same pleasure. I was delighted that Gordon seemed to sense my pride and share it. I showed Grandma off to some of my friends, and they were impressed. But mostly I kept the doll to myself. It gratified me that she was there where I could look at her. Sometimes I'd take off fifteen minutes when no one else was around and just hold her and think about what her life must have been like.

It was as if I'd solved a problem when I finished the doll. As if I'd found something missing, filled a hole somewhere deep in my being. My Grandma doll is a talisman; somehow she gets me back in touch with a part of myself that I'd lost. I can't explain it; dolls are just important to Turtle Delaware women, I guess.

People must have been impressed by Grandma; gradually her fame spread. Some of my friends asked me if I'd make dolls for them. I thought, why not? It's something I'm good at, something that gives me pleasure. So for several years I became a maker of dolls as well as the keeper of my Grandma doll.

In all, I must have made about twenty dolls. Many of them were old women in ribbon dresses. I even gave some of them gold earrings and clay pipes. I guess I wanted people to think they were getting Grandma dolls. But I never worked on those faces the way I worked on the first one. I want to make it plain that only one doll really was Grandma; the rest were only old Delaware women. I studied nineteenth-century costuming; it got so I became more interested in costume than in likeness or personality. I dressed my dolls in buckskin, in elaborate ribbon skirts and jackets. I started to make younger women, even an occasional man. I enjoyed making the dolls; I enjoyed the praise I got for them. But none of these later dolls meant anything to me, really. Not like Grandma.

I gave most of my dolls to friends. One I donated to the Questors, a charitable society in Dewey; I gave a little talk before the group, and they accepted my doll with great courtesy. It's found a home in the restored Dewey Hotel, which has become a local museum. I got to know a professional dollmaker who was passing through our part of the country; she admired my old lady dolls and traded me out of one of them.

The best part of the reception my dolls received was that people in Chicago, who didn't know anything about me, really took to them. By this time Linda was pretty well known in Chicago's Indian art world. She got my dolls exhibited in a local museum and at several art shows, and she tells me that people were intrigued. That suited me fine, but even better was that Linda herself was fascinated. She asked me all sorts of questions about how I made them. I knew it was a matter of time before she'd try her hand at dollmaking too.

My own work came to an end. My Parkinson's gives me the shakes so bad that I can't make the little features and fingers anymore. I don't really mind. I got what I needed from my time as a dollmaker. In my mind, I recovered the Delaware dolls from the grave where time, and Grandma, had consigned them. I reconnected with Grandma Wahoney and the long line of Turtle women who had passed on the dolls—and Delaware culture with them—for generation after generation. I became, in my own modest way, a Keeper of the Delaware dolls.

AFTERWORD

Well, there it is: my life, certainly the greatest part of it. We've walked familiar paths, driven back roads, followed some of the gossamer threads in my web of memory. It's down on paper now, maybe changed a little in the telling, but close, I think, to the truth of things. It's a modest story, as I told you it would be, but not without interest, I hope, for all that.

My life has been lived to old rhythms played by a country fiddle and an Indian drum. There's no jazz to it, no rock and roll. If that's what you want, you probably haven't made it this far in my narrative. I think that America has forgotten the sweet melodies you can get from a fiddle, the heart-pounding beat of an Indian drum. I'm hoping to remind folks about square dances and stomp dances: the simple things that have been important to me.

You know, when you're living your life, you're too busy with the day-to-day to see the patterns. When you get older, it's like you reach the top of some sort of hill. You can look back from a distance and see where you've been, what the path looks like, what some of the patterns are.

I've come to believe there are purposes, there are pathways through the world, that involve more than one life. As I look back, all the way back to Grandma Wahoney, who was Keeper of

the Delaware Dolls, and then at my own Grandma doll and at
the wonderful Apache Gan dancer dolls that Linda has brought
up to show me, I think I see such a purpose. We are linked by
ancient traditions; we are linked by motives that I, at least, don't
completely understand. But I know that the traditions and the
motives that bind us have power.

Grandma, who tenderly watched over her dolls, dressed them,
decorated them, freshened their hair, fed them, carried them to
the dance for so many of the long years of her life, apprehended
their power. Mama, who lost them, felt the pain of their ab-
sence. I, who found myself making an image of Grandma in
a carefully sculpted, neatly dressed little doll, felt their power
without quite understanding it. Linda, whose big, handsome
Gan dolls, shrouded in black, have helped me feel the mystery of
firelit Apache ceremonies, is also captivated by the magic of dolls.
Four women, whose lives span two centuries and more, bound
together by some obscure purpose involving the mysterious
power of dolls.

From my own experience, I believe the Delaware Doll Dance
must have influenced the health of the tribe. I think my own
dollmaking concerned my spiritual health, my own connection
with a past that was more important to me than I'd admitted to
myself. I see that my daughter has used her dollmaking to explore
the Apache traditions that are a vital part of her own heritage.

When Grandma Wahoney, despairing of the future, had her
dolls buried with her, I think she misjudged the world. The legacy
of many centuries is not so easily disposed of. Cultures are more
resilient, tradition has a stronger hold on us, for all the styles that
change. The buried dolls come back, in different forms, to lend
their healing power to new generations. We are each of us in our
own way, myself and my daughter, spiritual heirs of the Keeper
of the Delaware Dolls.